Surviving the Angel of Death

The True Story of a Mengele Twin in Auschwitz

BY EVA MOZES KOR
and Lisa Rojany Buccieri

Tanglewood • Indianapolis

Published by Tanglewood Publishing, Inc.
© Eva Mozes Kor and Lisa Rojany Buccieri, 2009.
© Eva Mozes Kor and Lisa Rojany Buccieri, 2020.

Cover design by Vera Braga
Interior design by Amy Alick Perich

Tanglewood Publishing, Inc.
1060 N. Capitol Ave., Suite E-395
Indianapolis, IN 46204
www.TanglewoodBooks.com

ISBN: 978-1-939100-45-0

Printed in the USA by Gasch Printing, LLC.
10 9 8 7 6 5 4

Library of Congress Control Number: 2020940189

Library of Congress Cataloging-in-Publication Data

Kor, Eva Mozes.
  Surviving the angel of death : the story of a Mengele twin in Auschwitz / Eva
Mozes Kor and Lisa Rojany Buccieri.
     p. cm.
  ISBN 978-1-933718-28-6 (hardcover)
  1. Kor, Eva Mozes. 2. Zeiger, Miriam Mozes, 1935-1993. 3. Jews--Persecutions-
-Hungary--Juvenile literature. 4. Jewish children in the Holocaust--Hungary-
-Biography--Juvenile literature. 5. Holocaust, Jewish (1939-1945)--Hungary-
-Personal narratives--Juvenile literature. 6. Twins--Biography--Juvenile literature.
I. Buccieri, Lisa Rojany. II. Title.
  DS135.H93K673 2009
  940.53'18092--dc22
     [B]
                                      2009009494

DEDICATION

This book is dedicated to the memory of my mother, Jaffa Mozes, my father Alexander Mozes, my sisters Edit and Aliz, and my twin sister, Miriam Mozes Zeiger. I also dedicate this book to the children who survived the camp, and to all the children in the world who have survived neglect and abuse, for I wish to honor their struggle in overcoming the trauma of losing their childhoods, their families, and the feeling that they belong to a family. Last, but not least, this book is dedicated in honor of my son, Alex Kor, and my daughter, Rina Kor, who are my pride and joy.

—*EMK*

To Olivia, Chloe, and Genevieve: the reasons for everything. And to my sister, Amanda, for saving my life.

—*LRB*

PROLOGUE

The doors of the train car were thrown all the way open for the first time in many days, the light of day shining upon us like a blessing. Dozens of Jewish people had been crammed into that tiny cattle car as it rattled through the countryside, taking us farther and farther away from our home in Romania. Desperate, people pushed their way out.

I held tightly to my twin sister's hand as we were shoved onto the platform, not sure whether to be glad for our release or afraid of what was coming. The early morning air was chilly, a cold wind nipping at our bare legs through the thin fabric of our matching burgundy dresses.

I could tell at once that it was very early morning, the sun barely making its way above the horizon. Everywhere I looked there were tall, sharp, barbed-wire fences. SS patrols, *Schutzstaffel* in German, leaned out of high guard towers, aiming their guns at us. Guard dogs held by other SS soldiers pulled against leashes, barking and growling like a rabid dog I once saw on the farm, their lips foaming, their teeth flashing white and pointy. I could feel my heart pounding. My sister's palm clenched sweaty and warm onto my own. My mother and father and our two older sisters, Edit and Aliz, were standing right next to us when I heard my mother's loud whisper to my father.

"Auschwitz? It's Auschwitz? What is this place? It's not Hungary?"

"We are in Germany," came the reply.

We had crossed over the border into German territory. In actuality, we were in Poland, but the Germans had taken over Poland. Germany's Poland was where all the extermination camps were. We had not been taken to a Hungarian labor camp to work but to a Nazi extermination camp to die. Before we had time to digest this news, I felt my shoulder being pushed to one side of the platform.

"*Schnell! Schnell!*" Quick! Quick! SS guards ordered the remaining prisoners from the cattle car out onto the large platform.

Miriam pulled herself closer to me as we were jostled about. The weak daylight was blocked and unblocked as taller people were first jammed up next to us, then pulled away by the guards to one side or the other. It looked like they were choosing some of us prisoners for one thing and some for another. But for what?

That's when the sounds around us began escalating. The Nazi guards grabbed more people, pulling them to the right or to the left on the selection platform. Dogs were snarling and barking. The people from the cattle car started crying, yelling, screaming all at once; everyone was looking for family members as they were torn away from one another. Men were separated from women, children from parents. The morning erupted into pure pandemonium. Everything started moving faster and faster around us. It was bedlam.

"Zwillinge! Zwillinge!" Twins! Twins! Within seconds, a guard who had been hurrying by stopped short in front of us. He stared at Miriam and me in our matching clothes.

"Are they twins?" he asked Mama.

She hesitated. "Is that good?"

"Yes," said the guard.

"They are twins," replied Mama.

Without a word, he grabbed Miriam and me and tore us away from Mama.

"No!"

"Mama! Mama! No!"

Miriam and I screamed and cried, reaching out for our mother, who, in turn, was struggling to follow us with her arms outstretched, a guard holding her back. He threw her roughly to the other side of the platform.

We shrieked. We cried. We pleaded, our voices lost among the chaos and noise and despair. But it didn't matter how much we cried or how loud we screamed. Because of those matching burgundy dresses, because we were identical twins so easily spotted in the crowd of grimy, exhausted Jewish prisoners, Miriam and I had been chosen. Soon we would come face to face with Josef Mengele, the Nazi doctor known as the Angel of Death. It was he who selected those on the platform who were to live and those who would die.

But we did not know that yet. All we knew was that we were abruptly alone. We were only ten years old.

And we never saw Papa, Mama, Edit, or Aliz again.

CHAPTER ONE

Miriam and I were born on January 31, 1934, in the village of Portz in Transylvania, Romania, which is in Eastern Europe near the border of Hungary and the beautiful Carpathian Mountains. The scenic countryside is still dotted with small villages, and life hasn't changed dramatically since I was a child, compared to much of the world. There was no running water or electricity, and people traveled by horse and wagon; a mode of transportation that some people still use in present-day Romania. The village was run by a notary who acted something like a mayor.

Both my father and mother came from Jewish families. It was rare for people to marry outside of their faith. In those days, marriages were arranged, and my father sent some friends to other villages to find prospective wives. According to the practice then followed by most Hungarians and Romanians, the friends put on their best clothes and carried a stick with a flower on it. If a marriageable woman was willing to meet the man, they took the flower off the stick. My mother accepted the flower, and friends and family made marriage arrangements, after which my mother finally met my father. My father was a fairly nice-looking man and wealthy for our area and time. My mother was only twenty-three years old, but that was considered ancient to be unmarried, practically an old maid. After they married, they decided to settle on my father's vast farm, most of which he bought from his brothers and sisters.

Miriam and I were identical twins, the youngest of four sisters. My sister, Aliz, had pretty green eyes and jet black hair. She was very artistic and sang beautifully. My other older sister, Edit, was the kindest sister that anyone could have asked for. She would pick us up from behind and twirl us around in circles for as long as we wanted.

To hear my older sisters grudgingly tell the story of our birth, you would have known immediately that we two were the darlings of the family. What is sweeter or cuter than identical twin girls? But I was born in the wrong place, at the wrong time, the wrong gender, and the wrong religion.

From the time we were babies, our mother loved to dress us in the same clothes, putting huge bows in our hair so people would know right away that we were twins. She even seated us on the windowsill of our home; passersby thought we were precious dolls, not even real people.

We looked so much alike that Mama had to put tags on us to tell us apart. Aunts, uncles, and cousins visiting our farm liked to play guessing games with us, trying to divine who was who. "Which one is Miriam? Which one is Eva?" a puzzled uncle would muse with a twinkle in his eye. My mother would smile proudly at her perfect little dolls, and my two older sisters would probably groan. Regardless, most people guessed wrong. When we were older and in school, we would use our identical twinship to trick people, which for us could be so much fun. And we took advantage of how precious and unique we were whenever we could.

Although Papa was strict and admonished us and our mother about the perils of excessive vanity, emphasizing that even the Bible warned against it, Mama particularly cared about our appearance. She had our clothes custom made just for us, ordering beautiful fabric from the city. When it arrived, she would take Miriam and me and our two older sisters, Edit and Aliz, to the house of a seamstress in the nearby village of Szeplak. There, we girls were permitted to hungrily peruse magazines featuring models wearing the latest styles. But our mother made the final decision on the cut and color of our dresses, for in those days girls always wore dresses, never pants or overalls like boys. Always our mother chose burgundy, powder blue, and pink for Miriam and me. After we were measured, we would set a date for a fitting and when we returned, the seamstress had the dresses ready for us to try on. The styles and colors of the dresses were always identical, two pieces made into one perfect, matching pair. The last dresses she made would save our lives.

Other people may have been baffled by our identical twinship, not being able to know who was who, but our father could tell Miriam and me apart by our personalities.

By the way I carried my body, a gesture I would make, or the second I opened my mouth to speak, it was clear to him who was who. Although my sister had been born first, I was the leader. I was also outspoken. Any time we needed to ask Papa for something, my oldest sister Edit would encourage me to be the one to approach him.

My father, a religious Jew, had always wanted a boy. At that time only a son could participate in public worship and say *Kaddish*, the Jewish mourner's prayer, upon someone's death. But Papa had no son, only my sisters and me. Since I was the younger of the twins and his last child, he often looked at me and said, "You should have been a boy." I think he meant to say that I was his last chance at getting a boy. My personality didn't help: I was strong and brave and more outspoken—just like he must have imagined a son of his might have been.

This stronger personality of mine, while setting me apart, also had its downside. It seemed to me that my father believed everything about me was wrong; nothing I did appeared to please him. Many a time we would argue and debate, and I was not willing to give in. It was not enough of an answer for me that my father was right just because he was a man and my father and the head of the household. So we always seemed to be disagreeing, Papa and I.

I definitely got more attention from him than Miriam or my other sisters, but it was not always the kind of attention I wanted. I never learned to skirt the edge of the truth with little white lies, so I was always in trouble. I can recall tiptoeing around the house to avoid my father sometimes, as I am sure he often tired of me and my big mouth.

Looking back, however, I realize that my battles with Papa toughened me up, made me even stronger. I learned to outsmart authority. These battles with my father unwittingly prepared me for what was to come.

My mother was very different from my father. She took us shopping in our best horse and buggy, and she read to us from story books. She loved to sing and would always do so when she ironed, a habit I adopted in my own adult life—it made a tedious chore much more pleasant. She would give us garden plots and create a contest for which plot produced the best vegetables. It was a great motivator to keep us trying to do better, to work harder.

Mama was quite educated for a woman of those times, because not all women got to go to school. Especially among religious Jews in those days, girls and women were mostly expected to take care of the home and the family, while the education and studying was reserved for the boys. And while my mother made sure that we learned to read, write, and do math, along with studying history and languages, she also taught us to care for others in our community.

We were the only Jewish family in Portz, our village, and were friendly with everyone. My mother was the kindest person I ever knew. She heard all the town news and often assisted our neighbors, especially young pregnant mothers in times of need. She would take them noodles or cake, help them with the household if they were sick, give them advice on raising children, and read them instructions or letters from other family members. She taught me and my sisters to follow in her lead, serving those less fortunate, especially since we were better off than many other people in our small farming village.

There were always community events in the village. Some were work events, and we always helped. In the fall, there would be corn-husking parties. At other times, villagers would gather in the barn to beat seeds from sunflowers. We would tell each other stories and share the latest village gossip. There were also frequent dances, when local musicians played in barns, often ours. If a stranger came through town and had no place to stay, we always offered a room at our home.

Yet almost from the time we were born, antisemitism pervaded our country of Romania. That means that many people around us did not like Jewish people just because they were Jewish. We children were never aware of the antisemitism until 1940, when the Hungarian army came.

My father once told us of an antisemitic incident that happened to him in 1935 when Miriam and I were just one year old. In that year, the Iron Guard—a violent, antisemitic, political party that controlled the village offices, the police, and the newspapers—stirred up hatred against Jews by making up false stories about how evil Jewish people were, and how Jews wanted to cheat everyone else and take over the world. My father and his brother, Aaron, were thrown into jail by the Romanian Iron Guard on fake charges of not paying taxes. It was all a lie; they had always paid their taxes. They were singled out and arrested just because they were Jewish.

Papa told us that when he and Uncle Aaron got out of jail, they decided to go to Palestine to see if they could make a living there. Palestine, at the time, was an area of land in the Middle East where the Jewish people lived before their exile during the time of the Roman Empire; especially during periods of persecution, it was always thought of as a homeland by many Jews. A part of Palestine had been settled by Jewish immigrants early in the twentieth century, and it eventually became the independent state of Israel in 1948.

My father and Uncle Aaron stayed in Palestine a few months and then came back to Romania. Upon their return, Uncle Aaron and his wife sold all their land and possessions and planned to emigrate, or move.

Papa urged Mama to leave and settle in Palestine, too. "It's good there," he said. "The country is warm. There are plenty of jobs."

"No," she protested. "I can't move with four small children."

"We need to leave now, before it gets worse here for us," urged my father, who was worried about the news he was hearing of increasing persecution of the Jews all over Hungary throughout other countries in Europe.

"What would I do there? How would we manage? I have no desire to live in the desert," said my mother. And like mothers sometimes do, she put her foot down and refused to go. I often wondered what our lives would have been like had she relented.

In our little village in Romania, we lived in a nice house on a vast farm. We had thousands of acres of crops: wheat, corn, beans, and potatoes. We had cows and sheep, from which we produced cheese and milk. We had a large vineyard and produced wine. We had acres of orchards, giving us apples, plums, peaches, and juicy cherries in three colors: red, black, and white. In the summer, those cherries became our beautiful earrings when we pretended we were fancy, dressed-up ladies. Mama also loved her flower garden in front of the house and her vegetable garden in back, and her cows, chickens, and geese.

But what concerned her most was leaving behind her own mother. We children loved to visit Grandma and Grandpa Hersh. And my mother, as an only daughter, felt responsible for taking care of Grandma Hersh, who was not in the best of health and often needed Mama to look after her.

"Besides, we are safe here," said my mother. She really believed that the rumors of Jews being persecuted by the Germans and their new head of state, Adolf Hitler, were just that: rumors. She saw no need to flee to Palestine or America, places of safety for Jewish people like us. So we stayed in Portz.

Portz, a largely Christian village of one hundred families, had a minister. The minister's daughter, Luci, was our best friend; both Miriam and I loved playing with her. In the summer we climbed trees in the orchard, read stories, and put on plays in a little theater we made by stringing up a sheet between two trees. In the winter we even helped Luci decorate her Christmas tree—we did not tell our father because he would not have approved. Our friendship also added to our feelings of safety. We were best friends with the Christian minister's daughter. How could we be persecuted in our own home town?

Though rumors of Jews being deported to labor camps began to spread here and there, Mama did not believe we were in danger. Even when we heard of the new ghettos—restricted areas of European towns where Jews were forced to live so they could be controlled in squalor and poverty—we did not believe we were really in any danger. Even when Jews were stripped of all possessions, all freedoms, sent away to labor camps and driven to work for no pay like slaves, we did not think it could happen to us. We never thought they would come to our tiny village in the remote countryside, far from any city.

One of my early memories is of the men of a Jewish labor camp from Budapest who came through our village. The Hungarian government would bring these slave laborers out of the camp to work on the railroads; when the work was completed, the laborers were taken back to the labor camp. While working on the railroad, they had nowhere to stay at night, so my father let them all sleep in our barn. Sometimes their wives would come to visit and stay in our house. In return, the women brought us lots of toys and, more importantly, lots of books from the city. We children spent hours lost in the worlds of those books. I could finish a book in a day. Because of them, I developed a love of reading at a young age.

As I understood only later from the books I read on World War II, Adolf Hitler came to power in Germany as the head of the Nazi party in 1933. Hitler hated Jews as much as the Romanian Iron Guard did, and leaders of the antisemitic and racist parties became allies, joining together in their hatred and their designs to rule all of Europe. Then in September 1939, World War II began when German Nazi troops invaded Poland. The Hungarians, under the leadership of Miklós Horthy, also trusted Hitler and became allies. All this began to happen around us, but still far enough away from us that only Papa fretted about our safety.

But in the summer of 1940, when Miriam and I were six years old, things changed. Hitler gave the northern part of Transylvania to Hungary. At that time the population in Transylvania, the larger area surrounding our village, was half-Hungarian, half-Romanian, but everyone in our village was Romanian. Rumors spread that the Hungarian army would kill Jews and Romanians and set our village on fire. Even as a six-year-old child, I knew we were in danger.

Miriam, the quieter of the two of us, felt my anxiety, must have seen it on my face and in my body language. But she never complained; it was not her nature.

One day about 6:00 in the morning, we saw the Romanian army withdrawing from our area. Shortly, our town crier banged his drum and announced, "Hear ye! Hear ye! The notary asks all of the villagers to go to the top of the hill to welcome the Hungarian army." It was strange. One army withdrew and another took its place. Not one shot was fired.

In a cloud of dust, Hungarian soldiers marched into our village, the commanding officer leading the troops in a long, shiny black car. The small parade was impressive, as it was intended to be. We villagers were to take note: The Hungarian army were now in power, so we were to *welcome* them! We heard the soldiers singing, "We are Horthy's soldiers, the best-looking soldiers in the world."

The commander demanded to speak with someone. Nobody spoke Hungarian except our family.

"I will speak with you," said my father.

"We will stay in the village," said the commander. "We need someplace to stay." No one volunteered to let the soldiers stay with them.

Finally, my father said, "We have a large yard and house. You can stay with us.

That night, the soldiers camped in our yard; the commanding officer slept in our guest room—the only Jewish house in the village. I have a feeling that they knew we were Jewish, but nothing was said about it. There did not seem to be any problems because we were Jewish—at least that night.

Mama treated the officers like company: She baked her best chocolate torte and invited the officers to dine with our family. I remember that there was much conversation about good food, and Miriam and I were excited to sit at the table with these important men in uniform. It was a pleasant evening, and the officers praised Mama's cooking and baking. Before they went to sleep, they kissed her hand as they thanked her, a courtly habit of many European and Hungarian men of the time. Early the next morning, they left, and our parents seemed to be reassured.

"See?" said Mama. "There is no truth to the talk that they are killing the Jews. They are real gentlemen."

"Why would people tell such stories?" Papa asked, not expecting an answer, much less disagreement from my mother or anyone else in the family. "It seems you are right. Nazis will never come to a small village like ours," he concluded. This we were to take as fact. Papa had said it.

Yet late at night, behind closed doors, our parents listened to a battery-operated radio. They discussed the news in Yiddish, a language they had purposefully not taught us so they could speak of things they didn't want us to know. What was it they were hearing that would be so secret, something so bad they tried to hide it from us girls?

I pressed my ear against the door and eavesdropped, trying to hear what was happening. "Who is Hitler?" I asked when they came out.

Mama brushed off our questions with blithe reassurances: "You don't need to worry about anything. Everything will be fine." But we had overheard some of the radio broadcasts with Hitler yelling about killing all the Jews. As if we were bugs!

Children are very sensitive to their surroundings, the atmosphere, though adults always think their children are unaware of things that they aren't told. We *felt* there was trouble, no matter how much our parents tried to reassure us otherwise. Their secretive behavior made it worse; even Miriam became anxious. We were always worried, even as young children. There was a disquiet about the unspoken, the undiscussed.

Persecution of Jews had become an open government policy with the arrival of the Hungarians, and people were rewarded for harassing us. We learned what that would mean in the autumn of 1940, when Miriam and I started school.

Unlike elementary schools today, our schoolhouse had children from first grade to the fourth grade in one room. Miriam and I were the only Jews. We were also the only twins. Every day we wore matching outfits to school and the same color ribbons tied at the ends of our long braids. Like our family had before them, our new classmates enjoyed figuring out which twin was which.

We also discovered we had two new Hungarian teachers at school who had been brought in from the city by the Nazis. To my surprise, they brought with them books containing slurs against Jews. The books also showed cartoon caricatures depicting Jews as clowns with big noses and bulging bellies. And marvel of marvels, for the first time, we saw "jumping pictures" projected on the wall—which is what we called early motion pictures because we did not know what a film was. I clearly remember watching the short film called "How to Catch and Kill a Jew." These propaganda films, shown before feature films in the theaters in cities, were something like today's commercials and previews but were designed to produce hatred of Jewish people. Imagine watching instructions on how to kill Jews right before a Pixar movie!

Watching the hate movie and reading the new books inflamed the other students. Our friends, or other children who had been friends, started calling Miriam and me names like "dirty, smelly Jews." Their name-calling really made me angry. Who were they to call us dirty? I knew I was as clean if not cleaner than any of them! Kids began to spit at us and beat us up at every opportunity. One day, our math book contained this problem: "If you had five Jews, and you killed three Jews, how many Jews would be left?"

Upset and frightened, Miriam and I ran home crying. Our clothes were filthy from being pushed into the dirt once again, and our dusty faces were streaked with tears. "Children, I'm so sorry," Mama said, hugging and kissing us, "but there is nothing we can do. Don't worry! Just be good girls. Say your prayers, do your chores around the farm, and study your reading."

One day at school in 1941 some boys played a trick on the teacher when her back was turned. They placed bird eggs on her chair. The entire class knew they were there, but no one said a word. We all held our breath as she turned around and sat down. Of course, the second she sat, the eggs broke, spattering on her new dress.

"The dirty Jews did it," stated one of the boys in our class matter-of-factly.

"Did you?" asked the teacher, looking at Miriam and me.

"No, Madame Teacher, no!" We were horrified. We had never misbehaved like that or played a trick on a teacher. We would never have heard the end of it from our parents had we dared! And we loved school and loved learning.

And then it happened. "Yes, they did!" screamed the

other children. "They did it! We saw them!" It was as if they had all made a secret pact behind our backs beforehand, and this was the result.

Miriam and I protested, but to no avail. We were Jews, and we were guilty.

Without asking more questions, the teacher called us up to the front of the class for our punishment and threw dry corn kernels onto the floor. "Kneel!" she demanded, pointing to us. For an hour, she made us kneel on the corn kernels in front of the class. The hard kernels dug into the flesh of our bare knees. But that was not what really wounded us the most. What hurt most were our classmates taunting us, leering at us, making ugly, smirking faces at us. Miriam and I were as shocked as we were hurt.

We came home and told our mother. Crying and hugging us, Mama said, "Children, I am sorry. We are Jews, and we just have to take it. There is nothing we can do." Her words made me angrier than the teacher's punishment. I wanted to hit someone myself, pound something hard like those kernels into dry corn dust. How could Mama's words be true?

When Papa came in from farming at the end of the day and heard what had happened to us, his attitude was like Mama's. "Jews have been persecuted for two thousand years. We believed that if we tried to get along, we would survive," he said. "We must obey tradition. Just try to get along." Papa reasoned that since we were one Jewish family living in the middle of nowhere, the Nazis would not bother to come take us away.

My father, being a very religious man, reminded us that in other Jewish tragedies, God somehow performed miracles and saved the Jews. It is also important to note that human beings in general don't want to believe that anything awful will happen to them, but only to other people.

In the afternoon and evenings, the disturbances continued. Teenage boys who belonged to the Hungarian Nazi Party, but who were not yet eighteen years old—the age at which they could begin to serve in the military—often surrounded our house and shouted obscenities at us for hours. "Dirty Jews!" they yelled. "Crazy pigs!" They threw tomatoes or rocks that smashed right through our windows. Other villagers joined in. Sometimes this would go on for three entire days, with us unable to leave the house.

"Papa," I called, "please go out and make them stop!" I wanted him to *do* something!

"Eva, there is nothing we can do about it. So just learn to take it."

I could not have known it at the time, but Mama and Papa must have felt that if they tried to stop these juvenile delinquents or fight back, they would be arrested and taken away from us. To them, the most important thing was to stay all together as a family.

Miriam and I huddled together in our bed, frightened. Our sisters stayed away from the windows. I know they were scared as well.

Conditions grew increasingly worse. In June 1941, Hungary entered World War II as an ally of Jew-hating Adolf Hitler and Germany, his country. Jews in other places in Europe were forced to wear a yellow star of David—the Jewish star—on the outside of their clothing or on their jackets to let everyone know that they were Jewish. We were not required to wear the yellow star, but everyone knew that we were Jewish. We were increasingly isolated in our village.

Unlike many Jewish children in Europe, Miriam and I were still allowed to attend school with other non-Jewish children, although it was progressively more difficult for us there, as the teasing and taunting did not stop. Our lucky older sisters, Edit and Aliz, were tutored in German, art, music, drawing, math, and history—all the subjects required in high school—by a Jewish teacher who lived with us at home.

As the light of autumn darkened into early winter, the days became shorter and our lives became more constricted. We did not venture to play outside or go into the village as much as we used to. Our parents never shared their worries, but Miriam and I grew more and more afraid.

Then one night in late September 1943, Mama and Papa shook us awake. "Eva! Miriam!" they hissed urgently. "Get dressed! Put on your warm clothes, as many as you can get on, with your jackets and your boots. Do *not* light that candle! It has to stay dark. And be very, very quiet."

"Wha-what are we doing?" I asked sleepily.

"Just do as you're told!" murmured Papa.

We piled on our warm clothing and went into the kitchen. By the light of the glowing embers in the fireplace, we saw our older sisters standing there. They were bundled up as well, their faces like stones in the shadows.

Papa gathered the four of us girls together and whispered, "Children, the time has come when we must leave. We are going to try to get over the border to the non-Hungarian side of Romania where we will be safe. Follow us and remember: no noise."

Single file, with Papa in the lead and Mama at the rear, we slipped out of the house into the darkness. Outside it was cold and windy. But at the time I had only one thought: We were in trouble, big trouble. And we were running away from it.

Silently we walked, one behind the other, to the back gate of our property at the edge of the orchard. Just beyond the gate lay the railroad tracks. No trains passed at night. It was silent except for the sounds of the crickets and the occasional call of a night bird. If we were to walk along the tracks for an hour or so, we knew we would arrive at the safe part of Romania. When Papa reached the gate at the edge of our property, he leaned over to unlatch it and pushed it open.

"Stop!" shouted a voice. "If you take another step, I'll shoot!"

A Hungarian Nazi youth pointed a gun at us. A group of teenage boys wearing Hungarian Nazi armbands with swastikas and khaki caps had been guarding our farm, stationed there to make sure we did not get away. We didn't know how long they had been watching us, there to prevent us from leaving.

We were only six Jews. How could we be so important? I clutched Miriam's hand, not daring to look directly at them, but sneaking sideways glimpses at the soldiers. Papa closed the gate, and the boys marched us right back to our house.

Our only chance of escape had just vanished.

For much of my life, I resented my parents for hiding what was happening. But this, too, like my father's sternness, prepared me for what was to come. I learned that I could not always trust adults to tell the truth, especially if the truth was bad.

CHAPTER TWO

On January 31, 1944, Miriam and I would turn ten years old. On family birthdays, Mama had always baked a cake and made the day a fun and festive occasion. But Miriam and I never got to celebrate our tenth birthday. Mama was too sick. Since October, just after the teenage Nazis had prevented our escape, she had been ill with typhoid fever and stayed in bed all winter. In those days there were no simple medicines to ease the pains of fever and illness like there are today in every pharmacy. We worried about her and whether she would get better. Our mother had always been so strong and healthy.

Our father hired a Jewish woman from another village, Șimleu Silvaniei, to care for her. We were not allowed in the room with Mama, but I remember watching from the doorway as my father would help my mother move and turn— she was so very weak. I was surprised at how gentle he was, his tenderness. Edit, Aliz, Miriam, and I helped by doing more than our usual share of chores on the farm.

The Nazis and the Hungarian authorities were watching us, but we were never under house arrest or forbidden from leaving our home. For the moment, we seemed safe. We even continued to attend school, except on the rare days the Nazis did not allow us to go. On those days we were tutored at home like our older sisters.

Our relative freedom came to an abrupt end one morning in March, that year we turned ten. Two Hungarian *gendarmes,* or policemen, arrived in our front yard. Soon they were pounding on the door.

"Get your belongings! Gather them up. You are going to be moved to a transportation center." This was not a request; it was a command. "You have two hours to pack."

Mama barely had the strength to get out of bed. Papa and our older sisters bundled up food, bedding, clothing—all the necessities they could think of. Miriam and I wore matching dresses and took two other sets of identical clothes.

As the policemen marched us out of our home, everyone in Portz watched us leave on the one road that ran through the village. Neighbors came out of their farmhouses and lined the road. Our classmates from school just stared. No one tried to stop the *gendarmes* from taking us away. No one said a word.

I was not surprised. Once word got around that we had tried to leave in the middle of the night, conditions had continued to get worse; the harassment from the villagers and their children had grown uglier and more frequent.

Even Luci, our best friend, stood very still, her eyes not meeting ours as we approached her house. She did not say she was sorry nor give us anything to remember her by to take on our journey. Just before we passed her house, I glanced at her. She looked down. In silence we left the home we had always known.

I felt hurt for many years about that day, believing the villagers didn't care about us. But I have taken several trips to Romania in recent years, long after WWII. I found Luci still living in the Portz area, and she still felt like a friend to me. I also met up with older Portz villagers who also expressed sadness at what had happened to our family.

On a later trip, I finally had a chance to ask Luci about that day we were taken away. She told me she burst into tears when she heard my family and I were taken by Nazis. While we were marched out of the village, she said she kept thinking and hoping an adult would stop them, but no one did. Looking at me being taken away felt unbearable, so she looked down. I understand now that there was nothing our remaining friends in the village could have done. Anyone who tried to help us would have most certainly been shot.

Bundled into a horse-drawn, covered wagon, the policemen took us to Şimleu Silvaniei, about a five-hour ride away. Once there, we were forced to stay in a ghetto with more than seven thousand other Jews from our Romanian area of Transylvania. Miriam and I had never seen so many people. To us, one hundred people—the number of neighbors in our village—was a crowd. Seven thousand people—all of them Jews!—were more than we had ever seen at one time in our entire lives.

We later learned that Reinhard Heydrich, chief of the main security office of the Third Reich, Adolf Hitler's main office, had issued an official order: All Jews in Nazi-occupied areas were to be moved to certain areas set aside for them; these special places were called ghettos. We had not heard about these ghettos before. Ghettos were areas enclosed by fences, walls, or barbed wire, and they were set up in the most run-down sections of cities or the poorest parts of the countryside. Jews were forbidden to leave without a special permit, even to buy food or medicine, upon penalty of death.

Our ghetto was located in a field enclosed by a barbed-wire fence that looked as though it had been quickly built. The Berretyo River ran through the middle of the field. The only building was an abandoned brick factory, which the commandant, or main security officer, occupied as his head-quarters. There were no tents or cabins or other structures in which Jews could take shelter or sleep. The commandant reassured us that this was very short term and we would soon be taken to work in labor camps in Hungary and remain there until the end of the war. "No harm will come to you," he promised.

Miriam and I helped Papa and our older sisters build a tent on the damp ground out of the sheets and blankets we had brought. We struggled and huffed while the ghetto commandant strode back and forth with his hands on his hips shouting, "Isn't it nice that I get to see the children of Israel living in tents like in the days of Moses?" He laughed uproariously as if he had told himself the funniest joke on earth.

Our entire family stayed in the same tent. Every time the sky darkened and it began to rain, the commandant barked through a loudspeaker, "Take down the tents! I want them to be built now on the *other* side." There was no logical reason for this except simple cruelty or perhaps to weaken us to make their future plans easier. By the time we took down our tents, crossed the bridge, and set up our shelter again in the mud, we were soaked.

Mama was still very weak from her illness, and living outdoors in the rain and cold just made her worse. At night Miriam and I slept close together, our small bodies giving each other warmth and comfort.

During our stay, the head of each family was taken to the headquarters for interrogation. One day, German guards came for Papa and took him away for questioning. They believed my parents were hiding gold and silver or had concealed valuables at our farm; they wanted to know exactly where. But Papa was a farmer and his only riches were his land and the crops he produced. He told the guards he had no silver except our Shabbat, or Sabbath, candlesticks. Four or five hours later they carried him back to our tent on a stretcher. He was covered with whip marks, oozing blood. They had burned his fingernails and toenails with the flame of candles. It took him many days to recover.

Miriam and I felt helpless. We were still children and expected our parents to take care of us. But there was nothing they could do to make it better for us. And there was nothing we could do for Papa, who was still suffering from the beatings and torture he had endured.

Our older sister, Edit, took charge of the cooking. We had been told to bring two weeks' worth of food when we came, but Mama had us girls bring everything we could carry—beans, bread, and noodles. As the weeks went by, we rationed our food and ate beans once a day. Sometimes non-Jewish people came to the edge of the ghetto and threw in food and other supplies, but I do not remember if we ever got any of that to eat.

Finally, Mama had realized just how bad things really were for our family. Miriam and I complained about sleeping on the wet ground and about that gnawing ache in our tummies all the time, but Mama could no longer help us as she used to do. She sat on the ground, shaking her head over and over again. "It's all my fault," she said. "We should have gone to Palestine." Her eyes, sunken by her illness and with dark circles under them from lack of proper sleep, showed that she was haunted by her decision not to flee to Palestine with Uncle Aaron when they had the chance. Now, trapped in the squalor and deprivation of the ghetto, she grew increasingly withdrawn and depressed.

On a morning in May, 1944, German guards told us we were going to a labor camp, which they said was in Hungary. "This is for your own protection. If you work you will live," they said. "Your families will stay together." We had heard rumors circulating among the grownups in the ghettos that Jews sent to Germany would be killed. So we thought that if we stayed in Hungary, we would be all right, we would be safe.

The guards told us to leave our belongings, that everything we would need would be at the labor camp. Nevertheless, Mama and our older sisters took a few valuables from our tent. Papa carried his prayer book. Miriam and I put on our matching burgundy dresses.

The guards marched us to the train tracks and herded us into cattle cars, pushing and shoving until one car was packed with eighty or one hundred people. The guards made Papa responsible for our car. Papa was told that if anyone escaped, he would be shot. The doors were slammed shut and sealed with a metal bar that slid into two handles. Barbed wire covered four small windows up high, two on each side. How could anyone escape?

Miriam and I pressed close together. There was no room to sit or lie down, not even for young children like us. Even though I was just a little girl, I could sense that something awful was about to happen. Just seeing our parents so powerless—parents who I had always seen as our protectors, no longer able to give us protection—had ended the last sense of any safety.

For days our train rushed along the tracks, the endless sound of the clacking interrupted only by an occasional hoot of the train's horn. Not only did we have no place to sit or lie down, we had no food or water, and no bathrooms. I remember being very thirsty, my mouth pasty and dry.

When the train stopped for refueling on the first day, Papa asked the guard for water. The guard demanded five gold watches in exchange. The grownups gathered the watches and handed them over. Then the guard tossed a bucketful of water toward the barbed-wired window. Water splashed in uselessly. I don't remember anyone getting a real drink. I may have had a drop or two, but that did not begin to quench my thirst. The second day, the train stopped again, and the same thing happened with the water.

One person died in our car during our journey. At the next stop, Papa decided to ask the guard to remove the body.

"Guard," he called. "Guard."

"What do you want, you dirty Jew?"

"Someone died in here. Can you remove the body?"

The guard just laughed.

At the end of the third day, the cattle car stopped, and Papa, speaking Hungarian, asked a guard for water. Someone answered in German, *"Vass? Vass?"* What? What? He had not understood Papa.

Then it hit us: We were not in Hungary anymore. We had crossed the border into Poland, now German territory.

A feeling of horror took hold of us. Up until then, there was hope. Everybody, including me, had understood that as long as we stayed in Hungary, there was some chance that we would go to a labor camp to work. Everyone knew by now that Germans and Germany meant death to Jews. Many people started praying. The cattle car filled with the sound of adults barely stifling their crying, children feeding off their exposed despair. Here and there someone attempted to chant the *Sh'ma*, the Hebrew prayer to God to hear us, to save us.

The train began moving again. Miriam and I were quiet as it gathered speed, going faster and faster. We had gone three days without food or water.

On the fourth day, the train stopped. Papa called out again to the guard for water. No one answered.

We realized we must have arrived at our destination. I stood on tiptoes to look through the window. I could only see the barbed wire in the window and dark gray sky. We heard lots of German voices yelling orders outside for an hour or two. The doors stayed closed.

Dawn finally came, time for Papa to say his morning prayers. He took out his prayer book and tried to figure out which direction was east, because Jewish people pray to the direction of Israel, which is in the Middle East. I wondered how he could pray at a time like this.

As Papa and others prayed to God, I felt angry—anger I had felt before: when we were called "dirty Jews"; when we were punished at school for problems we hadn't caused; when we were not given a travel pass to visit our grandmother; when the Nazi boys prevented our escape; when no one spoke up or helped us as we were marched out of our village. Why did my father think praying would help?

"Papa," I said, "we don't know where we are. They have lied to us. We are not at a work camp."

"Eva, we must pray to God for mercy," said Papa. "Come to me." He pulled our family into a corner of the cattle car. Miriam and I squeezed close to him, and our sisters and Mama followed. We listened quietly to our father as he spoke. "Promise me that if any of you survives this terrible war, you will go to Palestine where your uncle Aaron lives and where Jews can live in peace."

He had never spoken to us girls like this before, with respect, as though we were adults. Miriam and I and our older sisters solemnly agreed.

Papa began his morning prayers.

Outside I could hear German voices yelling orders. Dogs barked at us from every direction. The doors of the cattle car screeched open. SS guards ordered everybody out.

"Schnell! Schnell!" Quick! Quick!

I saw tall barbed-wire fences and cement guard towers everywhere. Soldiers were hanging out of them with the barrels of their guns pointed at us. I have no idea how we got from the cattle car to the selection platform. Miriam and I may have jumped or stepped down a wooden ramp. But pretty soon we were standing on the platform, feeling utter terror, two ten-year-olds in matching burgundy dresses.

CHAPTER THREE

Mama grabbed Miriam and me by our hands. We lined up, side by side, on the concrete platform. The smell hit me: a foul odor I had never smelled before. It reminded me of burned chicken feathers. At home on the farm, after plucking the chickens, we would singe off the last little feathers over a flame to clean it. But here the stink was overpowering. It was as if you walked through it, around in it. It was everywhere and inescapable. I did not find out right away what the smell really was.

This place was confusing and noisy.

People were yelling.

There were screams.

Confusion.

Desperation.

Barking.

Orders.

Crying, crying, crying. The crying of children for parents. The crying of parents for their babies. The crying of people confused and bewildered. The crying of people who saw with certainty that their nightmares had come true. All together, the cries resounded with the ultimate and most unimaginable pain of human loss, of emotional grief, of mental and physical suffering.

I felt disconnected, as though I was watching things happen to someone else. Here and there I glimpsed layers of barbed-wire fences, bright klieg lights, and rows of buildings. The SS guards strode among the groups of people, as if searching for something.

Suddenly I felt like I had landed in my body again. I looked around, and I felt Miriam's quaking frame next to mine. But where was Papa? And where were my older sisters, Edit and Aliz? I searched desperately, holding the hands of my mother and my twin. I could not find the rest of my family. After four days of such close proximity to my older sisters and Papa, in my bewilderment and confusion I had lost them.

I never saw them again.

I tightened my hold on Mama's hand. An SS guard rushed by. He was calling out in German, *"Zwillinge! Zwillinge!"* Twins! Twins! He barreled past us, then stopped short, whirled around, and came back. He stood in front of us. His eyes traveled back and forth from Miriam's face to mine, up and down our matching burgundy dresses.

"Are they twins?" he asked Mama.

She hesitated. "Is that good?"

"Yes," said the guard.

"They are twins," replied Mama.

Without one word, he grabbed Miriam and me, tearing us away from Mama.

We screamed and cried as we were dragged away. We begged him to let us stay with her. The German guard paid no attention to our pleas. He pulled us across the railroad tracks, away from the selection platform. I turned my head and saw my mother, desperate, her arms outstretched toward us, wailing. A soldier grabbed her and threw her in another direction, and my mama disappeared into the crowd.

That was the last time I ever saw my mother.

And that is also the last time I remember crying in Auschwitz. My childhood ended that day, that moment.

Then everything happened quickly, so quickly. Guards separated people on the selection platform into groups. One group had young men and women. In another, children and older people. Miriam and I held on to each other as we were brought to join a group of thirteen sets of twins who had come from our train transport: twenty-six children, all frightened and confused.

A guard brought a mother and her twins to stand with our group. I recognized her! It was Mrs. Csengeri, wife of the storekeeper in Şimleu Silvaniei, the town near our village. Her twin daughters were eight years old, and when we shopped at her store, she and Mama liked to talk about the problems of raising twins. She and her girls stayed with our group. Why had the guards let their mother come with them and not ours with us? I did not have time to ponder the question much before things started happening again.

After half an hour, an SS guard led us to a big building near the barbed-wire fence. As soon as we entered the building, we were ordered to undress. I felt numb again, not part of my own body. This was all a nightmare, right? It would end the second I opened my eyes, and Mama would be there to comfort me, right? But I was not dreaming.

All of us were given short haircuts. The barber explained that twins received privileged treatment: While other prisoners had their heads shaved, we were allowed to keep some hair. Luckily, I had learned some German, so I could understand what was being said on a basic level. As I watched our long braids fall to the floor, I did not feel so very privileged. We were thirsty, hungry, and exhausted. Our father and sisters had disappeared, and we had been wrenched from our mother. And our problems were very far from over.

Next we took showers. Our clothes had been fumigated with some sort of anti-lice chemical and were returned to us. Wearing our own clothes was another "privilege" twins received that other prisoners did not. Miriam and I put on our dresses, but now each had a big red cross painted on the back. I instantly hated that red cross on my dress. Wearing the dress did not feel like a privilege. I knew that like the yellow star they forced Jews to wear in the ghettos, the Nazis were using that red cross to mark us so that we could not escape.

Right then and there I decided not to do anything the guards asked me to do. I would give them as much trouble as possible. In the processing center, prisoners' arms were being tattooed. We watched as the prisoners went up one after another, were told to hold out their arms, which were then pinned down while the instrument seared numbers into their flesh with acute pain.

Not me. I was angry, and I was not going to be a sheep anymore. When my turn came, I struggled and kicked. The SS guard grabbed my arm. The feel of his grip twisting my skin dissolved my resolve. "I want my mama!" I screamed.

"Hold still!" ordered the guard.

I bit his arm. "Bring back my mama!"

"We will let you see her tomorrow."

I knew he was lying. They had just torn us away from Mama, so why would they reunite us the next day? Four people had to hold me down while they heated the point of a pen-like gadget over an open flame and dipped it into blue ink. Then they held the hot pen to my flesh and began to burn my number into the outer part of my left arm: A-7063.

"Stop!" I yelled. "That hurts!"

I squirmed and wriggled so much that they could not hold me completely still. Because of my struggling, the numbers on my arm were blurred.

Next they tattooed Miriam. She did not struggle like I had. Her number was A-7064. The tattoo on her arm was clear.

Our arms felt painful and swollen as we were marched across the camp to our barracks, where we would reside. Along the way I saw groups of skeleton-like people accompanied by SS guards with huge dogs. The prisoners were returning from work. What kind of work did they do that made them so thin? Were they sick? Did they not get food? Everything around me stank with that horrible, thick, chicken-feather smell and looked dark, gray, and lifeless. Threatening. I do not remember any grass, trees, or flowers anywhere.

Finally we arrived at our barracks in Camp II B, the girls' camp in Birkenau, also referred to as Auschwitz II. The building was a barn originally built for horses. It was filthy. The stink inside was worse than the stench outside. There were no windows on the lower part of the walls for light or ventilation, only across the top above our heads, which made it suffocating. A double row of bricks forming a bench ran down the middle of the barracks. At the end stood a three-hole latrine, another privilege for twins; we did not have to go outside in the big public latrine to go to the bathroom. There were a few hundred twins from ages two to sixteen. We spotted Mrs. Csengeri's daughters there, too, but we did not speak to them at that time.

That first night a pair of Hungarian twins who had been there a while showed us the triple-decker bunks. Miriam and I had a bunk on the bottom.

When the evening meal arrived, all the other children rushed to the doorway. Dinner consisted of a two-and-a-half-inch slice of dark bread and a brownish fluid that everyone called "fake coffee." Miriam and I looked at each other. "We can't eat this," I said to one of the Hungarian twins.

"It's all you will get until tomorrow," she said. "You had better eat it."

"It's not kosher," I said. At home on the farm, we only had kosher food—food that fulfilled the requirements of Jewish dietary law—that Papa blessed before every meal.

The twins laughed at us, but it was not a kind laugh, more like a boy-are-you-stupid laugh. And they greedily wolfed down the bread that Miriam and I offered them.

"We're glad to have the extra bread," they said, "but the two of you are going to have to learn to eat everything if you want to survive. You cannot be fussy, and you cannot worry about whether or not something is kosher."

After the meal the Hungarian twins and some of the others briefed us. "You are in Birkenau," they told us. "It is part of Auschwitz, but it's three kilometers from the main camp. Auschwitz has one gas chamber and one crematorium."

Miriam said, "I don't understand."

I asked, "What is a gas chamber? What is a crematorium?"

"Follow us, and we'll show you." The twins led us to the back of the barracks near the door where the barracks supervisor did not notice us. We looked up at the sky and saw flames rising from chimneys that towered over Birkenau. Smoke covered the whole camp and fine ash filled the air, making it as dusky as the sky after an explosion of a volcano—it was that thick. Again, we were hit by that terrible smell.

Even though I was afraid to ask, I heard myself saying, "What are they burning so late in the evening?"

"People," said a girl.

"You don't burn people!" I said. "Don't be ridiculous."

"The Nazis do. They want to burn all the Jews."

Somebody else said, "Did you see how the Nazis divided the people arriving on the trains into two groups this morning? They are probably burning one group right now. If the Nazis think you are young and strong enough to work, you are allowed to live. The rest are taken to the gas chambers and gassed to death."

I thought of Mama who was so weak after her long illness.

I thought of Papa, clutching his prayer book.

I thought of our two older sisters.

Deep down I knew, without being told, that they had been pushed into the line that had gone to the gas chamber. Against that feeling, I allowed myself to hope that maybe they were still alive. After all, they were older and smarter than Miriam and me.

"We are children," I said. "We can't work, but we're still alive."

"For now," replied a twin. "And it's only because we're twins, and they use us in experiments conducted by Dr. Mengele. He'll be here tomorrow right after roll call."

In a quavering voice, I asked, "What experiments?"

Lea, a twelve-year-old twin, told us to stop worrying and go to bed.

All of the children slept in their clothes and shoes, so Miriam and I did, too. We lay in our wooden bunk on a straw mattress in our matching dresses. Although I was tired, I could not sleep. Tossing and turning, I noticed something moving on the floor. "There are mice in here!" The scream came out of me without my thinking about it.

"Quiet!" someone said. "Those are not mice, they are rats. They won't hurt you if you don't have any food in your bed. Now go to sleep." I had seen mice before on our farm, but they were not huge like these rats; these rodents were the size of small cats.

I needed to use the latrine and so did Miriam. In the dark, we put our feet down, slowly, carefully, because of the rats. We kicked our shoes back and forth to scare them away. Then we hurried to the end of the barracks. The latrine was about twelve feet square, with dark wooden walls and a cement floor. These latrines were not like latrines today; there were not toilets or even seats. Our latrine floors had holes in them that you had to perch over. They were even worse than the rest of the barracks. Vomit and human feces that had missed the holes of the latrine were everywhere. The smell was hideous.

We stepped inside and I froze. There on the floor in the filth were the dead bodies of three naked children. I had never seen a dead person before. There they lay, on that hard, cold, stinking floor . . . dead.

At precisely that moment, I realized that Miriam and I could die, that we were in a place where that happened. I made a silent pledge to do everything in my power to make sure that Miriam and I did not end up dead like those children. We were going to be stronger, smarter, *whatever it took* not to end up that way.

From that point forward, in my mind, I always visualized Miriam and me walking out of the camp alive. I never permitted fears or doubts to dominate my thoughts. As soon as they entered my mind, I pushed them out forcefully. From the moment I left the latrine, I concentrated all my being on one thing: how to survive one more day in this horrible place.

CHAPTER FOUR

In the morning a whistle shrieked. It was still dark. "Up! Up! Up!" shouted the barracks supervisor, a *pflegerin*, or nurse, who took care of us. She wore a white coat. "Get ready!" she screeched.

Miriam and I did not know the routine yet. Holding hands we watched the older girls helping little ones prepare for roll call. Outside we lined up in rows of five to be counted. Roll call took half an hour to an hour. Everyone had to stand for roll call—winter, summer, rain or shine, whether a toddler or a teen. No one was excused for any reason. Even the dead were brought to roll call.

Looking back, I do not remember a single child sitting down or crying. Not even the two-year-olds. I think we understood instinctively that our lives depended on cooperation.

After roll call, we went inside to straighten up the barracks. The three dead children Miriam and I had seen at the latrine the night before were no longer on the floor. We learned that when a child died, the other children in the same bunk could not stand lying next to a dead body, so they removed the corpse to the latrine and kept her clothing for themselves.

As for the three dead bodies Miriam and I had seen, adults had put them back into their bunks to be counted.

In addition to roll call, every day, every child had to be counted, dead or alive. Dr. Mengele knew how many twins he had, and no corpse could be disposed of without following procedure.

That first morning an SS guard waited at the front of the barracks. "Doctor MENGELE is COMING!" she yelled. The supervisors seemed nervous, twitchy with anticipation of the great man. Miriam and I stood at attention, not daring to move and half-holding our breath.

Dr. Josef Mengele entered the barracks. He was dressed elegantly in an SS uniform and tall, shiny, black riding boots. He wore white gloves and carried a baton. My first thought was how handsome he was, like a movie star. He strode through the barracks, counting twins at every bunk, with an entourage of eight people accompanying him. We later learned that the group included a doctor named Konig, a girl who was the interpreter, and several SS guards and assistants. Mengele was never escorted by fewer than eight in his entourage at these barracks checks.

When Dr. Mengele stopped at the bunks containing the three dead bodies, he flew into a rage. "Why did you let these children die?" he screamed at the nurse and SS guards. "I cannot afford to lose even one child!"

Our nurse and the supervisors trembled.

He continued counting until he came to Miriam and me. He stopped and looked at us. I was petrified. Then he moved on. The other children told us that he had been on the selection platform the day before when we had arrived. He was the one who made the selections of the prisoners with a flick of his baton. To the right meant the gas chamber, to the left, the camp and forced labor. Both paths ended in death, whether quickly in the gas chambers or a slow death by starvation, cold, and brutal demands made on laborers.

After Mengele left the barracks, we received our morning food rations. Miriam and I drank the fake coffee, although it tasted awful. Most importantly, it was made from boiled water, and we soon learned that meant it was safe and would not give us dysentery—endless diarrhea.

In groups of five, we marched from Birkenau to the labs in Auschwitz. We entered a big two-story brick building. Miriam and I were forced to take off our dresses, underwear, and shoes. There were boys as well as girls: twenty or thirty sets of twins. In the beginning I was shocked at the sight.

I found out later that boy twins stayed in a separate barracks under better conditions than ours. They were cared for by a young Jewish prisoner, formerly an officer, named Zvi Spiegel, whom Mengele had chosen to supervise them. Zvi intervened to help the little boy twins, convincing Mengele to give them better food and to improve their living conditions; Mengele must have realized all this would make them better guinea pigs. So Zvi, also known as the "Twins' Papa," comforted the boys, gave them games to keep their minds active, and taught them bits of geography and math. During the day he would let them kick around a soccer ball made of a bundle of rags to keep them in better physical condition. He also had them memorize each other's names to make them feel human.

We had no such person in our barracks to lead us and help us form friendships. I never went up to another girl and asked her name or told her mine. We were all alone, just twins with numbers, each of us trying to survive. The only person I had to think about was Miriam. I gradually stopped thinking of my family at all.

In that brick building, as I looked around, I noticed some fraternal twins, but most were identical like Miriam and me. Later I learned that Dr. Mengele wanted to discover the secret of twinning. One goal of his experiments was to learn how to create blond-haired, blue-eyed babies in multiple numbers to increase the German population. Hitler called Aryans, the blond and blue-eyed, white-skinned Germans "the Master Race"—and we were his human guinea pigs. To study other natural "abnormalities" and to try to figure out how to prevent genetic mutation, Mengele's research included giants, dwarfs, the handicapped, and gypsies. The dwarfs lived in barracks near ours, and we sometimes saw them walking through camp.

In the lab, it was very cold. All of us sat completely naked on benches, both boys and girls together. It was embarrassing to be there without any clothes. We had no place to hide. Some girls crossed their legs and covered up with their hands. Others shook with fear while SS guards pointed at us and laughed. The nudity was one of the most dehumanizing things in the camp for me and the worst part of being a Mengele twin.

Dr. Mengele popped in and out to supervise. Other doctors and nurses in white coats who were inmates or prisoners like us observed us and took notes.

First they measured my head with an instrument called a caliper, made of two pieces of metal, which they pressed against my skull and squeezed. The doctor called out the numbers to an assistant, who wrote notes into a file.

They measured our earlobes; the bridges of our noses; the size of our lips; the width, shape, and color of our eyes. They compared the shade of blue of Miriam's eyes to the blue of my eyes with a chart of eye colors. Over and over they measured. They spent three to four hours on one ear. Each time the doctors measured me, they measured Miriam to see how we were alike and how we were different. A photographer snapped pictures; an artist drew sketches. Technicians took X-rays, five or six at a time.

Next they asked us questions and gave commands. An inmate who spoke Hungarian and German acted as translator. If I did something, Miriam did the same. "Every time I follow you," Miriam whispered, "they write something down. They want to see which of us is the leader." Of course it was me, just as it had always been. After observing us the previous day in the processing center when I had resisted tattooing, they also knew I was a troublemaker.

We sat there for six to eight hours. I hated every second. Finally we were allowed to get dressed and were marched back to our barracks for the evening meal: a meager portion of very dark bread, about two-and-one-half inches long.

In the afternoon our supervising nurse made us learn a song in German. It went, "I am a little German child. If not, phooey!" She put us in a circle and made one girl stand in the center. We had to walk around that girl and sing, "Phooey, phooey, phooey!"

"Dirty, filthy Jews!" the nurse shouted at us. "Swine!" She loved that song. It meant we children were disgusting.

We hated that nurse. We called her "Snake" behind her back. She had thick legs and long black hair that she wore in a braid. Snake kept taunting us. "Who do you think you are?" she asked.

We did not answer. She did not expect an answer, either.

"You think you are so smart because you are still alive?" asked Snake. "You're going to be dead before long. We're going to kill all of you."

For the first day or two, Miriam and I cried and cried. But we soon realized that crying would not help anything. We mostly felt numb.

Staying alive was the most important thing. We knew we were alive because of the experiments. Because of a fortunate accident of nature.

Because we were Mengele's twins.

Chapter Five

Being in Auschwitz was like being in a car accident every single day. Every single day something terrifying happened.

Within two weeks of arriving in Auschwitz, Miriam and I had to have our heads shaved. Like all the twins in our barracks, we were infested with head lice. Head lice, I learned, lay their eggs on human hair, and they can travel from one head to another. The only way to get rid of them is to use a special shampoo or chemical treatment and comb hair daily with a fine-toothed nit comb. We had none of these things, so lice multiplied and spread from person to person, onto clothing and bedding—they nested in our blankets, straw mattresses, and dresses. We were constantly scratching ourselves, and Miriam and I constantly picked lice off each other and tried to squeeze them dead between our fingernails. But there was no lasting relief. Even with our hair chopped off and all our efforts, we still had lice.

Once a week, twins had the privilege of taking a shower. Forty or fifty twins showered at the same time. Each of us received a bar of soap. In the huge shower room, we took off our clothes and left them in a pile to be disinfected. Later I learned that the chemical used to disinfect our clothing, Zyklon B, was one of the three chemicals used to gas people to death at Auschwitz. The Nazis combined Zyklon B, which came in gray-blue pellets, with hydrogen cyanide and diatomite to form the chemical mix for mass murder in the gas chambers. The gas, mixed with burning flesh and bones, created that stench I noticed the first day. It is not a smell a human can ever forget.

Miriam and I stayed close. We always stayed close. Before we washed, we stood in a tub of whitish liquid. It burned my legs and left red blotches. Sometimes the supervisors wiped down our heads and bodies, and the disinfectant stung my eyes. Dr. Mengele wanted us to be clean and did occasionally have his assistants make attempts to clean up our barracks. Yet the filth and lice from the camp would always return, and we coped with it as best we could.

One time we saw some boys at the shower. I remember looking at them and thinking, "They're so skinny. I'm glad I don't look like that." Actually, I probably *did* look like that. Miriam too. Her eyes were sunken, and I could count every bone in her body. But I did not feel skinny and pathetic. I needed to see myself as strong.

Dr. Mengele set up a routine for us to follow. On Mondays, Wednesdays, and Fridays, we were forced to march to the labs in Auschwitz for intensive studies that left us exhausted. Tuesdays, Thursdays, and Saturdays were spent in the blood labs in Birkenau. One day melded into the next.

Every morning after roll call, Mengele came to our barracks for inspection. Smiling, he called us *meine kinde*, my children. Some of the twins liked him and called him Uncle Mengele. Not me. I was terrified of him. Even in those days, I knew he did not care about us like a real doctor.

In the blood lab, Miriam and I sat on a bench with another set of twin sisters. Someone tied both of our upper arms with thin, flexible, rubber hoses. Two people worked on me at the same time. A doctor jabbed a needle into my left arm to take blood. He withdrew a vial's worth and then stuck me again. I could see hands taking away bright red vials of my blood. I remembered wondering, "How much blood can I lose and still live?" Meanwhile a different doctor gave me an injection of something in my right arm. He stuck five needles in without removing the first one. What was he shooting into my remaining blood?

I hated shots. But I refused to cry out in pain because I did not want to let the Nazis know they were hurting me. I coped by turning my head away and counting the shots until it was over.

On our way back to our barracks, Miriam and I did not talk about the shots. I saw those shots as the price we had to pay to survive: We gave them our blood, our bodies, our pride, our dignity, and in turn, they let us live one more day. I cannot remember a single twin who did not cooperate.

We didn't know what the experiments were for or what we were injected with. Later we found out that Dr. Mengele purposely gave some twins dangerous, life-threatening diseases such as diphtheria, then followed them with shots of something else to see if it cured the disease. Some shots were attempts to change the color of eyes.

Older girls, many years after we were all liberated, told us Mengele had taken them to a lab and given them a transfusion of blood from a boy, and had transfused their blood into the bodies of boys. He wanted to discover a way to change girls into boys and boys into girls. Many of these details I learned forty years later, such as the twin teenage boys who had some of their private parts cut off in Mengele's quest to see if he could turn them into girls. One of those boys died in his bed right next to his twin, who said later, "I could feel my brother's body turning cold."

It was said at the time that six sets of twins had gone to that lab and been killed. I never witnessed anyone being killed; I only knew that some of the twins disappeared. But I did eventually learn that the rumors were correct, that twins were dying from some of the experiments. We were told they had become "very sick." Then Mengele would simply replace them with fresh sets of twins who had just arrived on transport trains. That is how even the most privileged prisoners at Auschwitz were viewed. Not even Mengele's favorites were treated as humans. We were replaceable. Disposable.

What was not replaced were our pretty, matching dresses, which got so worn out we could no longer wear them. We were given women's clothing. But the clothing was too big, so Miriam and I tied strings around our waists to hold up the dresses. In the tops of our dresses we tucked anything we were carrying, like a metal cup or a piece of bread saved from the night before.

In the morning before roll call and on the days we went to the blood lab, we helped take care of the younger children. Outside our barracks we had a fenced-in yard where we played with them. The older girls taught Miriam and me how to knit. We pulled pieces of barbed wire from the fencing, hit the wires against stone to loosen the barbs, and pulled them off, which took a long time. Then we sharpened the points of the wire on some rocks to make knitting needles. One of the twins had an old sweater that we took apart, saving the yarn. Each girl took a turn knitting until the yarn from the sweater was all used up. Then the next person would unravel the yarn, and we would start all over again. It was not about a finished product—a cap, a scarf, or socks. Knitting took our minds off of our troubles.

But death and danger were never far away. One day when we were outside, a cart of dead bodies rolled by. We ran to the fence to see if we recognized any of the corpses.

One girl cried out, "Mama! It's my mama!" and burst into tears. She sobbed, her anguish growing into wails, as the cart continued on its way. I felt sorry for her, but I did not know what to say.

At that moment, I realized that maybe our mother had also gone by on a cart of bodies; we just hadn't seen her. Every day those carts went by. Sometimes the prisoners on them were dead, sometimes only mostly dead; regardless, they were all being carted away to their final resting place.

Until that moment I had stopped thinking about my family. Maybe it was due to the bread we ate each evening that supposedly contained not only sawdust but a powdered sedative called bromide that made us lose memories of home. Whether that was true or not, I could not feel sorry for myself, for Miriam, for anyone. I could not think of myself as a victim, or I knew I would perish. It was simple. For me, there was no room for any thought except survival.

At night Miriam and I lay in our bunk with two other sets of twins. We snuggled close but did not talk or whisper. If I had told Miriam how hungry and miserable I was, it would have only made things worse. In the darkness I heard a whistle, a car, or motorcycle going by. Noises of marching, moaning, vomiting, barking, and crying punctuated the hush of camp—an orchestra of the pervasive human misery.

Occasionally when our supervisors were asleep, our old friend from the neighboring village, Mrs. Csengeri, sneaked into our barracks to see her twin daughters. She was a smart, quick-witted woman. Upon her arrival at Auschwitz, she had convinced Dr. Mengele she could help him by giving him information about her twins, so she was allowed to stay in the women's barracks. Mrs. Csengeri brought her children food, underwear, hats, things she had taken or "organized." "Organizing" was camp language for stealing from the Nazis. I envied those girls for having a mother who was still alive and caring for them; Miriam and I had only each other.

I could not think about Mama, Papa, or our older sisters any more. I had to worry about Miriam and myself. I had to repeat to myself over and over:

Just one more day.

Just one more experiment.

Just one more shot.

Just please, please, don't let us get sick.

CHAPTER SIX

One Saturday in July we marched to the lab, where I was injected with something that must have been a germ. They gave the shot only to me, not my twin. Years later Miriam and I guessed they chose me for the shot because they had observed that I was stronger.

What I was not prepared for was that this injection would make me very ill. During the night, I ran a high fever. My head pounded. My skin burned dry. My body shook so hard, I could not sleep despite my fatigue. I woke Miriam.

"I'm v-very s-s-sick," I whispered through chattering teeth into her ear.

She was instantly awake, instantly worried. "What shall we do?"

"I d-d-d-don't know," I said. "L-l-let's t-t-try to hide it and pre-pre-pretend that I'm all r-r-r-ight."

By Monday morning when we stood outside for roll call, I was really dizzy. My arms and legs were covered with red patches and swollen to twice their size. They were so painful, I thought I would explode out of my skin. I shivered

1. Eastern Europe at the beginning of World War II.

2. Eva's journey.

3. Eva and Miriam Mozes, 1935.

4. Eva's parents, Alexander and Jaffa Mozes.

5. Top row (l to r): Aliz, Papa, Edit, and friend Luci.
   Middle: Eva, Mama, Miriam.
   Bottom: cousin Shmulik.

6. *Standing are cousin Magda, sister Edit, and cousin Aggi. Lying on the grass are cousin Dvora and sister Aliz. All of the girls in this picture died in the camps.*

7. *Portz, Transylvania.*

8. *Entrance to Auschwitz. The sign is in German and translates to: "Work makes you free."*

9. *Auschwitz selection platform.*

10. Auschwitz.

11. Inside the camp.

12. Picture of twins in lab.

13. Josef Mengele.

PAŃSTWOWE MUZEUM
32-603 Oświęcim 5

r Lagerarzt des   . 1 0.AUG.1944   Birkenau, 8. August 1944
L Auschwitz II.
(Frauenlager)

An das
Hygiene-Institut der Waffen-ϟϟ u.Polizei,
A u s c h w i t z.

Anbei wird Blutmaterial zur Untersuchung auf
Rest N, Na Cl., Takata-Ara, Vitamin C eingesandt:
1.H.Nr.A 5131   Malek Judith
2.   "   80912   Kohnstein Emilie
3.   "   A 7736 Malek Salomon.
4.   "   A 5771 Molnar Maria
5.   "   A 6035 Moskowicz Helena
6.   "   A 3626 Weiss Olga
7.   "   A 7063 Mozes Eva
8.   "   A 7259 Neuschloss Judith
9.   "   80913   Kohnstein Gisela.

Der Lagerarzt des
KL Auschwitz-II.
ϟϟ-Untersturmführer

14. *Original document showing that Eva's blood samples were tested for Urea Nitrogen, Sodium Chloride, Takata-Ara, and vitamin C. There are also documents showing tests for syphilis and scarlet fever.*

To Whom It May Concern:

I, Werner L. Loewenstein, M.D., a physician educated in Germany, resident of Terre Haute, IN, located in Vigo County, have translated a document from The Camp Physician of The Concentration Camp Auschwitz II.

The Camp Physician   Birkenau, August 8, 1944
Concentration Camp Auschwitz II
(Women Camp)

To The Hygienic Institute of The Army SS and Police,

A u s c h w i t z

Enclosed are blood samples for examination of Urea Nitrogen, Sodium Chloride, Takata-Ara, and Vitamin C.

A list of nine names follows-see attached document.

Signed by The Camp Physician
Concentration Camp Auschwitz II
Mengele (looks like Mengele's signature)
SS Sub Storm Leader

I certify that I have translated the above from the attached document, and that this is an accurate and true representation of what is contained therein.

Werner L. Loewenstein
Werner L. Loewenstein

State of Indiana
County of Vigo

Before me, the undersigned, a Notary Public in and for said County and State, this 18th day of April 1985 Werner L. Loewenstein personally appeared and acknowledged the execution of the above translation.

Witness my hand and Notarial Seal

Margaret Jones Cassell
Resident of Vigo County

My Commission Expires
July 13, 1988

15. English translation of document on facing page.

with chills. The sunshine warmed me up a little, and I tried desperately not to tremble so that the *pflegerin*, or nurses, would not notice I was sick. I did not want to be taken to the infirmary. On two occasions, a twin in our barracks had become sick and taken to the infirmary. They never came back. The matching twin had then also been taken away and they did not return either. We assumed both twins in a set were killed once one got sick. I could not let this happen to Miriam and me. Why should she die just because I might die?

Just before roll call actually began, the air raid sirens sounded a loud, piercing warning: we were going to be bombed. With shivering delight, I watched the SS guards run for cover as a plane with an American flag painted on one of the wings circled the concentration camp. "Look at these Nazis," I thought to myself, "the bullies of the world, running like scaredy cats!" I recognized the Stars and Stripes because our aunt, Papa's sister, lived in Cleveland, Ohio, and before the war she sent letters to us with stamps printed with the American flag.

Now the plane flew low and made a yellow smoke circle above the entire camp. Even in those days, we knew that the plane would not bomb inside the circle. More planes followed, and in the distance we heard bombs exploding. The American planes gave us hope. The planes meant that help was coming. Someday soon we would be freed and get to go home—if we could just stay alive long enough. We kids clapped; those were our moments of glory.

On our next visit to the lab, the doctors did not bother

to examine me. They called my number and took my temperature. I knew I was in trouble. Immediately two *pflegerin* put me in some kind of car or Jeep and drove me away. I did not even get to see Miriam before I was taken away. It was the first time in the camp that we were separated. Staying together, counting on each other, having another human being to really care about had kept us both from feeling so alone.

The nurses took me to the infirmary: Building #21, a filthy barracks close to the gas chamber and flaming chimneys. A putrid stench filled the air. Bunks three tiers high held people who were half dead. Row after row, they formed a sea of human beings dying a slow death. All of them were grown-ups. As I walked past, they reached out their bony fingers:

"Please!"

"Water! Water!"

"Food! Please! Anything?"

"Help me!"

They all seemed to be crying, unable to move. It looked like there were more hands reaching out than there could have been people. I can recall reading about a Valley of Death in the Bible; the infirmary felt like that valley. It was the worst place I had ever been.

I was put into a room with two older girls, Vera and Tamara. Each of the girls was the sister of another pair of twins. They had chicken pox, so they were not too sick. Our room was small, but only we three shared it—another privilege for twins.

That night the time for dinner came and went. We received no food ration.

"Why aren't they feeding us?" I asked. "We should be getting bread."

Vera said, "No one here gets anything to eat because people are brought here to die or are taken from here to die in the gas chamber."

"They don't want to waste food on the dying," said Tamara.

I cannot die, I told myself.

I will not die.

That night I was too sick to feel hungry. I found it hard to sleep without Miriam beside me, cuddling. In the dark I heard people moaning and screaming in pain. Their screams cut into me. I had never heard so many voices wailing, howling, and bellowing.

The next day a truck came. The sickest people were thrown onto the truck bed to be taken directly to the gas chamber. They shrieked and struggled as some of them were tossed on top of people who were already dead.

"Am I going to the gas chamber?" I thought. The gas chamber was always there, next to the crematorium, belching its stink of burning human hair, bones, and flesh into the air all around us. The gas chamber was a real possibility for any of us in that camp—but more so for those of us in the infirmary. Twice a week those trucks would come. Years later, I learned that right before the bodies were thrown into the crematorium, a group of workers would pull out gold teeth and remove any jewelry. The Nazis collected an average of seventy-six pounds of gold from the bodies every single day. Someone was getting rich.

The morning after I arrived, Mengele and a team of four other doctors came to see me. They discussed my case as though they were in a regular hospital. Although they spoke in German, I understood a lot of what they were saying. Dr. Mengele laughed and said about me with a smirk, "Too bad. She is so young and has only two weeks to live."

"How could he know that?" I wondered. They had not run any more tests on me after the poisonous shot. I've since learned that Mengele knew what disease they had infected me with and how it would progress. In all the years since, I have never found out for sure.

As I lay in the bed and listened to Mengele and the other doctors, I tried not to let on that I grasped the meaning of their words. At that moment I made a second secret pledge, "I am not dead. I refuse to die. I am going to outsmart those doctors, prove Dr. Mengele wrong, and get out of here alive." Above all, I knew I had to get back to Miriam.

During those first few days, I was running a very high fever, but no one gave me food, medicine, or water. They only checked my temperature. I was so thirsty, desperate for water, my mouth so dry I thought I could not breathe much longer.

There was a faucet at the far end of the barracks. I remember sliding out of bed, opening the door, and crawling on the floor to reach that faucet. The rough cement scraped my skin, chilling my belly. I stretched my hands forward and dragged my body on all fours, creeping slowly along that floor coated with muck and slime. Sometimes I passed out, then woke up and inched onward.

"I am going to get well," I kept repeating to myself.

"I must live. I must survive."

My thirst for water overpowered me. The strangest thing is that I do not remember drinking the water. I must have, because there was no other way I could have survived. I do not even recall how I got back to my bunk in the room I shared with the other girls. Yet every night for two weeks I pulled myself to that faucet.

After my first week in the infirmary, Miriam found out that I was not receiving any food. Mrs. Csengeri, our old friend, told her. Mrs. Csengeri acted as a messenger, sneaking from barracks to barracks as she visited her own twin daughters. Miriam started saving her bread for me and gave it to Mrs. Csengeri to deliver into my hands. Imagine Miriam's willpower, a ten-year-old deciding not to eat for a week! That daily piece of bread from my twin sister helped to save my life and made me more determined to be reunited with her.

After two weeks, like a miracle, my fever broke! I started feeling stronger. One night I woke up and saw the silhouette of our block supervisor: slim, dark. Every once in a while, she stole into our room at night and gave us food. "Here is a piece of bread for you," she said quietly, putting it on my bed. "If anybody finds out, I'll be punished." Once she even gave Vera, Tamara, and me a piece of her birthday cake.

What a treat! It was so good, so sweet. We devoured it, licking our fingers and then licking the paper that had held the cake. Even in Auschwitz some people were humane.

When I think back on those days, however, I am not sure why she did not give me water when I was so sick the first two weeks. I can only guess that she saved her efforts for those who looked as though they would survive.

As I gained strength I wanted to get out of that infirmary as quickly as I could, but I was still running a fever. Dr. Mengele and his team came twice a day to check my fever chart. I had to convince them that my temperature was going down so that I could be sent back to the twins' barracks. I thought of a plan.

Vera and Tamara taught me how to read the thermometer. When the nurse, a fellow prisoner, came in and placed the thermometer under my arm, she told me to keep it there until she returned. After she left the room, I took the thermometer out, read it, and shook it down a little. Then I put it back in my armpit almost all the way, letting it stick out the back so that it would not register any change. The nurse returned, read my temperature, and wrote it down. I had to be very careful to do this gradually so that Mengele would not get suspicious about my recovery.

The plan worked! Three weeks later I was released.

Joyfully I returned to my sister. Now that we were together, I knew I would get well. But I was shocked by Miriam's appearance. She had an empty look in her eyes and sat staring into space. She looked weak and lifeless.

"What's wrong?" I asked her. "What's happened? What have they done to you?"

"Nothing," said Miriam. "Leave me alone, Eva. I can't talk about it."

I knew that our separation had affected Miriam badly. She did not believe that I would come back; the thought of being all alone had made her lose hope. In camp language she had become a *musselman*, a zombie, someone who no longer had the spirit to fight for life.

For the first two weeks while I was gone she did not go to the lab. She was kept in solitary confinement, guarded by SS at all times. At first Miriam did not know what was happening to me, but my twin must have sensed they were waiting for something. When I did not die as Mengele expected, Miriam was taken to the labs and injected with many shots that made her sick. The shots would stunt the growth of her kidneys, keeping them the size of a ten-year-old's the rest of her life. I never discovered what she was injected with or the purpose of this experiment on my sister.

However, I did learn that Mengele had planned for me to die from the disease I had been given. Dr. Miklos Nyiszli, a Jewish prisoner and pathologist, wrote and published an eyewitness account about how Mengele routinely ordered pathologists to perform autopsies on twins who had died within hours of each other, a unique opportunity to compare the effects of disease on healthy and diseased bodies that were identical in most other ways. If I had died in the infirmary, Miriam would have been rushed to the lab and killed with a shot of chloroform to her heart. Simultaneous autopsies would have compared my diseased organs to her healthy ones. If the organs held any scientific interest, Mengele would have examined them himself and sent them on to the Anthropological Institute at Berlin-Dahlem in a package marked "War Material—Urgent."

However, I, a ten-year-old girl, had triumphed over Mengele by surviving his experiment. Now it was up to me to help my twin sister get better. I could not lose her. It was that simple. How to accomplish it was another thing.

CHAPTER SEVEN

At Auschwitz-Birkenau we never knew what tomorrow would bring. Each day brought challenges for us to survive. Miriam was very sick with something besides the incessant diarrhea of dysentery. Although everyone including me had dysentery, Miriam had given up the will to live. I had to find some way to help her to get better. Part of the reason she was so sick was due to the effects of the shots she had been given while I was away.

The word around camp was that potatoes would strengthen us and heal dysentery. In Auschwitz people "organized" anything needed for survival from the Nazis. Although Nazis viewed it as stealing, inmates viewed organizing as a victorious action. My problem was that I had never stolen anything before in my life except for one thing: a cup.

Once, on our way to the shower, as we marched in a row of five, we approached a pile of pots and pans. I edged from my place in the middle of the row to the outside. I leaped up, seized a cup, tucked it into the loose top of my dress, and marched on as though nothing had happened. If the SS guard accompanying us saw me, he said nothing.

Rumor was that anyone caught stealing would be hanged, just like those who tried to escape. The Nazis had made us watch these hangings before, telling us to observe closely, to see what would happen to us if we stole or tried to get away. I remember thinking to myself, "Yes, life is so wonderful here. Why on earth would we try to escape?"

I resolved to find a way to take some potatoes to help Miriam get well. I did not know what would happen to me if I dared to take potatoes, but I knew it could be death. A gibbet, the wooden frame for hanging people, stood in front of Block 11. Even if that was what awaited me if I were caught, for Miriam, the risk was imperative. I could not let my sister die.

Other twins in our barracks were cooking potatoes at night, so I asked them where I could get some potatoes. They told me the only place to get potatoes was the kitchen, so I volunteered to be a food carrier. This meant I would be one of two children hauling soup in a huge container the size of a thirty-gallon garbage can from the kitchen at the end of the camp to our barracks. It took twenty minutes to walk there; lugging back the heavy, filled can took us even longer.

The first time I volunteered I was not chosen. The next day I volunteered again and was picked along with another twin to get the daily soup, a watery liquid that occasionally had a bit of potato.

As soon as I entered the kitchen, I spotted a long metal table that held pots and pans. Beneath I noticed two sacks of potatoes. For a moment I hesitated. If I were caught, I could die, but if I did not try, Miriam would die.

I bent down and peered around to see if anybody was watching me. My heart pounding so hard I felt it in my ear canals, I reached into the sack and snatched two potatoes. Somebody grabbed me by my head and pulled me up. It was the kitchen worker, a fat woman prisoner wearing a striped scarf on her head.

"You cannot do that!" she yelled in my face.

"Do what, Madame?" My eyes were wide with false innocence.

"It's not nice to steal. Put those back."

I dropped the potatoes back into the sack. I expected to be dragged to the gallows immediately, but that did not happen. I almost burst out laughing with relief when I realized that my only punishment would be that scolding. I had just learned that being a Mengele twin meant that no one dared deliberately harm us as long as Mengele wanted us alive. He needed us to continue his experiments.

But I still had a worry that the kitchen worker would report my attempted crime to the *blocova*, our block supervisor, and I would not be allowed to carry food again. The next day, however, I volunteered and was chosen again.

This time it was easier to organize potatoes without getting caught. I was not nearly as nervous, because I knew the worst that could happen to me was a tongue-lashing.

Once I reached the sacks, I quickly grasped three potatoes from under the table and hid them in my dress. This time, no one saw. Success! That tiny cache of potatoes was one of the greatest treasures I had ever had. I could hardly *wait* for evening.

Any secret activities like cooking had to be done at night after the *blocova* and assistant supervisor had gone to bed in their little rooms at the front of the barracks. One of the twins had brought a few pieces of charcoal that she had organized during the day. We had an oven at the end of the brick bench that ran down the center of the barracks, and we made a small fire in it. Someone stood guard at the *blocova's* closed door in case she woke up. Other girls stayed at the entrance of the barracks and signaled by tapping their feet if anyone was approaching. In the dark we took turns cooking.

I used my own pot and boiled my potatoes and then Miriam and I had our feast—peels, spots, dirt, and all, with no salt or butter—but they tasted delicious to us. They filled us with warmth and raised our spirits. I would have given Miriam all of the food, but I was starving and needed strength to care for us both.

Every day after that, I volunteered to carry the vat of soup, though I was only chosen maybe one or two times each week. But with each turn, I became better at organizing. I always took more potatoes than we needed for that day. As a result, Miriam and I usually had potatoes three times a week.

Sometimes Mrs. Csengeri sneaked in at night and cooked the potatoes she had organized for her twin daughters. As soon as one person finished cooking, another took her place at the oven. We formed a little brigade and always had people posted on guard duty to make sure we did not get caught.

Everyone knew the system and the rules. Despite the fact that everyone was skin and bones, hunger reminding us we were still alive, we did not try to take one another's food.

The potatoes I brought Miriam worked like medicine. She became healthier, stronger, and willing to fight for her own life. I can say, and it would not have hurt her feelings, that my sister would have died then if it had not been for me. And in turn, taking care of Miriam had helped me become determined and more forceful, too. Because we were twins, we clung to each other. Because we were sisters, we depended on each other. Because we were family, we did not let go.

Over time, I could see that prisoners who had someone in the camp to care about— whether a relative, friend, or neighbor—were more likely to survive. The prisoners who had no one did not last.

At Auschwitz dying was so easy. Surviving was a full-time job.

CHAPTER EIGHT

As the summer of 1944 turned to autumn, things were changing. More and more airplanes roared overhead and bombed Nazi headquarters and factories. Sometimes there were two or three air raids a day. Although we had no radio or news, I think everyone in Auschwitz realized the good guys were coming to free us. I believe that if there had been no planes, many of the inmates would have died of sheer despair. It took effort to live in Auschwitz, and many might not have even tried to continue if not for the hope those planes brought.

I had to keep my twin sister and myself alive until they arrived. Her life was my mission and responsibility. But conditions in the camp were not better. In some ways, they were worse.

During the night of October 7th, the sound of a huge explosion woke us up. Sirens wailed. Dogs barked. What was happening? Later we found out that Jews of the *Sonderkommando* (prisoners forced to burn corpses of fellow prisoners) had rebelled and blown up Crematorium IV in Birkenau.

They used explosives smuggled to them by a group of Jewish girls working in the Nazi explosives factory. The men of the *Sonderkommando* decided they would rather go down fighting than die in the gas chamber. They wanted to take revenge for the deaths of families and friends.

Rumors circulated that as the Allied Forces—the American, British, and Soviet armies—approached, the SS would kill everyone in the camp. Nevertheless, Dr. Mengele continued his experiments, still hoping to make an important scientific discovery.

At that time we did not know that orders had come from the Nazi high command for Dr. Mengele to "liquidate" the gypsy camp consisting of more than two thousand prisoners, mostly women and children. Although Mengele had tried to preserve the gypsies for his research, he followed orders. They were taken to the gas chambers to be killed and then incinerated.

Miriam and I and all the twins in our barracks were marched from our camp to the gypsy camp, now empty. The inmates had left behind blankets and colorful paintings on the walls. We did not know why the Nazis transferred us to their camp. It was close to a gas chamber and crematorium, and the word went around that we were next to be gassed.

On that first day, we stood outside in the cold for roll call, patches of snow covering the ground, from 5:00 A.M. until 4:00 P.M. It was the longest roll call we had ever been through because a prisoner was missing. The smells of the crematorium were thick in the air, mixing with cold and fog.

My feet froze and so did my sister's. We never found out to where the prisoner had escaped.

For the next few weeks, we stayed in the gypsy camp, living in the shadow of the crematorium with constant dread that we would be killed. We never knew why that did not happen. Maybe we were saved by orders from Berlin to stop gassing the Jews. The Nazis by then must have known they were losing the war. Maybe they wanted to hide the evidence of their atrocities.

Then in early January, 1945, the SS began to order people out of the barracks to go on forced marches. "*Raus! Raus!* Out! Out!" they shouted. "Everybody out! We are taking you away for your own protection." We heard that thousands of people were now being marched deep into Germany.

"I am not going to leave the barracks," I said to Miriam. "I am not going on any march." I figured that the Nazis had not been particularly nice to us when they were winning the war, so they certainly would not be any nicer when they were losing it. We stayed.

To my surprise, no one came to get us. The Nazis were in such a hurry to get everybody out that they did not bother checking each barracks. Some of the twins remained with us, including Mrs. Csengeri and her daughters. At the time I did not know that many people had also chosen to stay behind.

The next morning, we woke up and realized we had missed roll call. We discovered that the Nazis were gone . . . or so it seemed. We saw no guards, no SS, no Dr. Mengele.

The joy and happiness we felt! The Nazis were gone! Now we were on our own. I spent my time trying to find food, water, and blankets to keep my sister and me alive.

One of the men prisoners cut an opening in the barbed wire so we could walk from one camp to another. Two girls and I went to search for things, roaming from area to area. I badly needed shoes. I was still wearing the ones from home that I had on when I had arrived at Auschwitz. The soles kept flapping open. I tied them with string, but it was still rather hard to walk. Miriam's shoes were in better condition because she had stayed in the barracks to guard our few belongings whenever I went out organizing.

The girls and I went to the place where the Nazis had kept all the clothes, shoes, and blankets they confiscated from the prisoners. It was a huge building the Nazis called "Canada," perhaps because they saw the country of Canada as a place of abundance. Piles of belongings rose to the ceiling. I rummaged through shoe after shoe after shoe, but I could not find any that fit, so I finally chose a pair that was two sizes too big. I stuffed the toe areas with some rags and tied them with string. At least my feet were now warm. I grabbed some coats and blankets for us and brought them back to the barracks where we bundled up.

One afternoon I went to the kitchen to organize food. A couple of kids and some grown-ups who had stayed behind were already there taking bread.

Holding four or five bread loaves in my arms, I heard the strange sound of a car. "The Nazis are gone, so whose car is coming?" I wondered. We ran outside to see. There was a Jeep-like car, and four Nazis holding machine guns jumped out and began spraying bullets in every direction.

I remember seeing a barrel of a gun pointed at my head, three to four feet from me, then I faded away.

When I woke up, I thought I was dead. All around me I saw bodies.

Okay, we are all dead, I thought. Then I tried to move my arms, and I could. Then I tried to move my legs, and I could move those, too. I touched the person beside me, but there was no movement. Her body was cold. Aha! *She* was dead, but I was alive!

I stood up, thankful to be alive. I thought it must have been a guardian angel that made me faint before the bullets hit me, because I did not have any time to think or do anything to save myself.

I raced back to the barracks. "Miriam?" I called as I burst inside.

There she was. "What happened?" she asked, eyes rounded with fear.

"The Nazis are back!" I said and added, "I wonder why they are back? They almost killed me!" I told her what had happened and how terrified I had been. "We don't have any bread. I was so frightened, I just ran for my life."

"Oh, Eva," she said, "what if you had been killed?"

We did not talk about that "what if" anymore. We just hugged and hugged.

That same night we were awakened by smoke and heat.

Flames shot down from the roof. We could feel searing heat from the flames through the barracks' walls. The barracks were on fire! We grabbed our stuff and ran outside. The Nazis were back at the camp, no longer in hiding, probably trying to destroy the evidence of their crimes.

Flames reddened the sky as far as we could see. SS guards had blown up a crematorium and the building called Canada. Shirts and dresses from Canada flew through the air amidst the sparks and ashes. The Allies were attacking and bombs lit the sky. It looked like the whole world was on fire.

Thousands of people surged out of the rows and rows of barracks. The same SS guards I had seen at the kitchen lined us up for marching. "Anyone who doesn't march quickly will be shot!" screamed a guard. He shot randomly into the crowd as a warning.

"Miriam, stay with me," I whispered. We did not know where we were going. I held onto her hand very tightly. We worked our way into the middle of the group. It was safer than being in the front or the back where we might attract attention. If they started shooting, we would be surrounded by other people.

The crowd swept us along. Being pushed and jostled in that big crowd, it was a struggle to stay in the middle. The SS kept shooting randomly as they herded us. As bodies fell to the ground around us, our fear increased. All of the children and the older people who had not been taken in the earlier marches were in this march. Later we learned that 8,200 people, including us, marched from Birkenau that night. In one hour, 1,200 were killed on the way. Only 7,000 people arrived at the barracks.

Forced by the wave of the crowd, we finally arrived back at the barracks in Auschwitz. It was still the middle of the night, but the brick buildings glowed in the klieg lights. Not knowing what would happen next, people started pushing hard, shoving to get inside the two-story building. Miriam and I also raced toward those barracks for shelter.

The SS guards inexplicably disappeared.

And somehow, I cannot remember how it happened, somehow in the shuffle I lost my twin sister.

"Miriam?" I called. "Miriam! Miriam! Where are you?"

I whirled around and around. She was not there, not anywhere!

As I began to panic, my heart clobbered in my chest, my breath rushed out of me in short bursts, my face burned hot despite the cold. My eyes, darting this way and that, filled with tears.

"What if Miriam winds up in another barracks?" I thought.

"What if she gets transported somewhere?

"What if she gets hurt?

"What if she dies? Who would know to tell me?

"What if I never see her again!"

I left the two-story building and half walked, half ran from barracks to barracks, calling her name. "Miriam! MIR-IAM! MI-RI-AM!"

I asked anyone and everyone whether they had seen a girl who looked just like me. "Her name is Miriam," I told them, "Miriam Mozes. Please, please. Have you seen a girl named Miriam?"

Some kind people must have seen my desperation, my panic. They helped me by joining in, yelling her name: "Miriam Mozes! Miriam Mozes!" But no matter where I went, no matter where I looked, no matter how loudly I yelled, I could not find her.

After a while, when Miriam did not answer, the people stopped helping me search. "Keep searching," they urged me, pity in their eyes, their own exhaustion making their bodies limp. "She has to be here somewhere."

"Miriam! Miriam!" I did not let thirty seconds go by without yelling her name.

While I saw pity and concern in some people's eyes, other people did not care, could not be bothered. Many of them were so beaten down, had suffered so much themselves, they did not have even an ounce of concern or energy left for anyone else. "So you're looking for your sister? Big deal! I don't have anybody."

I wanted to yell at them that Miriam was more than a sister. She was my other self. Our survival depended on each other! I could not stop to think about these hopeless souls. I had to find her. I had to.

I kept searching. "Miriam! Miriam!" I cried, my voice growing more hoarse, more faint. I was hungry and tired, but I did not allow myself to sit down to rest. I could not stop.

Terrified, I went from one building to another, unable to give up my search. So many emaciated people, their thin prison garb clothing their pitiful bodies, were blocking my vision everywhere I looked. They all looked the same to me because they were not Miriam. What could have happened to her? In one quick moment, dashing for safety, we had been separated! What had we done? I kept on.

My legs shuffling forward, my arms pumping to keep me moving, I did not let myself think of hunger, of the pains in my gut, of the dryness making my tongue stick to the roof of my mouth. None of it mattered. "Miriam! Miriam Mozes! Miriam!"

Hours and hours, minutes and minutes, seconds and seconds—all piled on top of one another in my panic. I had been searching for twenty-four hours. No Miriam! She could not have simply disappeared. I refused to accept that. Where was she?

I was stumbling about in a near-stupor of desperation and exhaustion when I went through yet another doorway.

"Miriam! Miriam Mozes! Miri—"

I bumped into someone about my height. "Sorry!" I was about to lurch past the person when it hit me: It was Miriam.

"Miriam! MIRIAM!" I fell into her arms. She fell into mine. "Where were you? I've been looking, looking, looking! What happened?"

"I have been searching for *you*!" she insisted. "What happened to you?"

We hugged, we kissed. Gripping one another we both slid to the floor to rest, crying and hanging onto each other.

"Eva, where were you?" she asked me through her tears.

"We made such a mistake by racing. I thought I would never see you again."

"No. I could not think too much about that. I had to find you!" I insisted. Then I admitted the truth to her. "I was desperate."

I sank into her arms, feeling like it was Hanukkah. It was a miracle!

I had the strongest feeling of relief and love that I have ever felt in my whole life. I pulled away to look at her scrawny face and then put my arms around her again, holding her tight. Those twenty-four hours of searching for her had felt like forever. The more I held on to her, the more I felt sure we would never be parted again. "I am so glad I found you," I told her, filled with more emotion than I could express.

Miriam reached out her hand. "Look!" she said. There she held a piece of chocolate. "Someone gave me this when I was searching for you."

My eyes opened wide. She offered it to me.

I broke it in half, and we savored it in this sweetest of moments.

"From now on, always hold my hand," I said. "Never let go."

Miriam agreed. "Yes, we must never be separated again."

"This is our lucky barracks!" I said.

"Then let's take a little nap here," Miriam said, sinking lower against the wall. "I'm so tired."

Our hands tightly entwined, our bodies close for comfort, we shut our weary eyes. No matter what happened next, we knew we had each other.

CHAPTER NINE

For the next nine days, Miriam and I were on our own, looking out for ourselves like everyone else was doing. We stayed in our lucky barracks with other sets of twins and adult women. My daily task was to find food for Miriam and me. Miriam's feet were frostbitten from that long roll call at the gypsy camp, so she protected our blankets and bowls while I went organizing with two other girls.

The girls and I broke into Nazi storage places and buildings where the SS had lived. Twice we went into Nazi headquarters, a nice house with nice furniture. Before that, I had not known such a place existed. Luxurious living right in the middle of a Nazi death camp.

We saw food on the table that looked awfully good. It looked freshly prepared, delectable! In fact, it looked too good. I wondered why the Nazis would leave such good food behind. Was something wrong with it? Out of hunger I snatched some up. But just before eating it, I stopped and put it back. Later I talked to people in the camp who said that the Nazis had purposely left poisoned food so that prisoners like me would eat it and die.

Another time, the girls and I found huge containers of sauerkraut. We ate the food, and since we had no water to drink and there was no snow on the ground to melt, we drank the sauerkraut juice. In the kitchen, we grabbed bread. For us it was a feast.

By this time we were skillful at scrounging for something to eat. I organized a scarf, and it became our most valuable tool. In a basement we came upon a huge pile of flour. I straightened out my square scarf and filled it with flour. Back in the barracks we mixed the flour with some liquid and baked a cake on top of the stove. It was like the Bible story of the unleavened bread the Jews ate when they had to leave Egypt in a hurry, with no time to allow the bread to rise. It was concentration camp Passover *matzoh*.

We still had very little food. I remember looking at my sister and thinking, "She's like a skeleton. Do I look like that, too?" Whenever we found something, we gobbled it up till it was gone. There was no such thing as leftovers. At that time, we did not know that stuffing ourselves in our starved condition was dangerous. Some of the girls became bloated, and one of my best organizing friends died from overeating.

One morning another set of twins and I set off for the Vistula River, which was not far from camp. Armed with a couple of bottles and containers, we planned to crack the ice, lower the bottles, and fill them with fresh water.

As I stood on the bank of the river, I saw a girl my age on the other side. She had braided hair and wore a nice clean dress and a coat. On her back she carried a school bag, so I knew she was going to school.

I froze. I could not believe there was still a world out there where people were clean and girls wore braids with ribbons and nice dresses and went to school! Once, I had been that girl in nice clothes with ribbons in my hair on my way to school. Until that moment, I thought everyone was in a concentration camp like us. But I realized then that was not true.

The girl stared at me. I looked down at myself wearing ragged clothes swarming with lice and a coat and shoes many sizes too big for me. I was hungry and scavenging for food and water. I do not know what she thought, but as I looked up again at her, I could feel the fire of anger rising in me. I felt betrayed. Miriam and I had done nothing wrong! We were just little girls like her. Why were we in this situation while she was over there looking so pretty and clean and living a perfectly normal life? It was so wrong, so inconceivable to me. But there she was. And there I was.

After what seemed like a long time, she hitched up her book bag and walked away.

I stared after her, watching her leave, then watching the empty space where she had stood. I did not understand it. I could not understand it.

Then I felt a grumble in my stomach, reminding me of my hunger and thirst. I found a thick stick and jabbed it angrily against the surface of the icy river, cracking it until the hole was big enough. I lowered my bottle into the frozen river, turned it slightly sideways, and watched the bubbles of air escaping as it filled with clear river water.

When we had collected as much water as our bottles would hold, the twins and I returned to the camp. Once there, we made a small fire and boiled the water to kill any germs.

I was very upset by this experience. The image of the girl stayed in my mind—as did all my questions about the outside world. I somehow reasoned that the world had let me down. It was not fair that this child was free and I was not. Although we made the trip to the river a couple more times, I never saw the girl again.

We could not leave the camp because battles raged all around us. It was dangerous to wander outside. Guns fired indiscriminately and hit anyone in the way. We were in the middle of a battlefield. In the noise and confusion outside, we learned to dodge the *rat-a-tat-tat* of machine-gun fire. If we heard a certain whining sound, we had to run for cover because a bombshell was coming in our direction. Bursts of gunfire flashed and crackled from the bunkers where the SS had gone to hide after dropping us off at the barracks.

During those days, rumors spread that the whole camp was going to be blown up—the barracks, gas chambers, and crematorium—to cover up evidence of Nazi crimes. The SS forced sixty thousand prisoners to leave on a death march. Miriam and I and many of the twins stayed huddled in our lucky barracks. Thousands of other prisoners, too old and sick to march, also remained.

Later I learned from an eyewitness account that on the night of January 18, 1945, Dr. Mengele had paid one last call to the lab where we twins had been measured, injected, cut into, and drained of blood so many times. He took two boxes of papers containing records of the approximately three thousand twins he had experimented on at Auschwitz, stashed them in a waiting car, and drove off to join a group of fleeing Nazi soldiers.

For about nine days we heard continuous shooting and bombing. The *boom-boom-boom* of artillery fire rattled the windows in our barracks. There was talk among the adults that we were soon going to be set free. Liberation. Miriam and I did not know what that meant. We hid inside and waited.

On the morning of January 27th, the noise stopped. For the first time in weeks, it was completely silent. We hoped this was liberation, but we had no idea what liberation would mean for us. Everyone in the barracks crowded at the windows.

It was snowing heavily. Until this day I only remember the camp being gray—the buildings, streets, clothes, people—everything dirty and gray. In my mind, a constant smoky pall hung over the camp.

On this day, sometime late in the afternoon, maybe about 3:00 or 4:00 P.M., a woman ran to the front of the barracks and started yelling, "We are free! We are free! We are free!"

Free? What did she mean?

Everyone ran to the doorway. I stood on the top step, huge flakes of snow falling on me. I could not see anything beyond a few feet in front of me. The snow had fallen all day, and the dirty gray of Auschwitz was now covered in a white blanket of snow.

"Don't you see something coming?" asked an older girl.

I kept peering through the swirling snow. "No . . ." I squinted.

Then I saw them.

About twenty feet away, we saw Soviet soldiers emerging through the snow, approaching us in snow-covered capes and suits. They did not speak as they crunched through the snow.

As they came closer, they looked to us like they were smiling. Were those smirks or smiles? I peered closely. Yes, they were smiles. Real smiles. Joy and hope welled up inside of us. We were safe. We were free!

Crying and laughing, we ran up to the soldiers, crowding them.

A shout rose from the crowd: "We are free! We are free!" There was laughter and wails of relief all mixed together in a jumble of celebratory sounds.

Laughing themselves, some of them with tears in their smiling eyes, the Soviet soldiers hugged us back. They handed us cookies and chocolate—delicious!

It was our first taste of freedom. And I realized that my silent pledge that first night in the latrine to survive and walk out of the camp alive with Miriam by my side had become a reality.

CHAPTER TEN

I threw my arms around the neck of a Soviet soldier, and he picked me up. I clung to him, with Miriam attached to my side. Everybody was hugging and kissing and shouting, "We are free!"

That night the soldiers continued the celebration in the barracks. They danced with the women and shared vodka with the men, right out of the bottles. Everyone laughed and sang. People pounded homemade drums using spoons on food tins, and someone played an accordion. Some of the children joined in dancing, jumping up and down on the floor, on the bunks, on the adults. I had never seen so much merriment, especially in our death camp.

Miriam and I sat happily on our bunk, watching and enjoying the scene of rare contentment and cheer. What a crazy sight. It was the pure human joy of being alive.

"We are free!" I mused aloud, nodding in time to the music.

"Yes. No more terrible *pflegerin!*"

"No more *Heil, Doktor Mengele!*"

"No more experiments!"

"No more shots in the arms!"

"No more hangings."

"No more . . ."

We were having a contest to list everything we would *not* miss now that we were free.

"We can do what we want!" Miriam said, satisfaction filling her tiny face.

Her words stopped me short. *We can do what we want.*

I watched everyone celebrating but did not see it. I heard the music and singing but did not listen to it.

We can do what we want. Whatever we want. We are free.

Memories of home filled my eyes. The sounds of the farm echoed in my ears: chopping wood, chickens clucking, cows bellowing. The smells of ripe fruits in the orchards filled my nose. I have no idea how long I sat there thinking.

It was Miriam who interrupted my reverie. "What is it Eva?" She shook my arm. "Eva! What?"

I turned to face her, my eyes finally adjusting to her presence. "Home," I stated. "I want to go home."

Miriam searched my face. "OK. We are free. Let's go home."

We took stock of our very few belongings, tucking them under us and into our clothing. That night we slept soundly for we had a plan: We were going home as soon as possible.

The following afternoon many Soviet people gathered around us. They asked Miriam and me and all the surviving children, most of them twins, to put on striped prison uniforms over our clothes. Because we were Mengele's twins, we had never worn those Auschwitz uniforms before.

I was already wearing two coats because it was so cold. Underneath our coats and dresses, Miriam and I carried everything we owned: food, bowls, blankets—things we regarded as treasures. We had naturally round faces, and with all the layers, we did not look like children who had been starving not long before, though we had been.

We stood at the very head of the line and held hands as Soviet soldiers marched us out of the barracks between the high, barbed-wire fences. A nurse holding a small child in her arms walked beside us. Huge cameras kept filming, filming. I looked at the cameraman and wondered why he was taking our picture.

"Are we movie stars or something?" I wondered. I was very impressed with it all. The only real movies Miriam and I had seen were the ones starring Shirley Temple that our mama took us to in the city.

To my surprise, after we had all walked through the fences, the cameraman sent all of us back inside and directed us to march out again. With nuns, nurses, and Soviet soldiers accompanying us, rows and rows of twins filed back into the barracks, then right back out again. We repeated the action several times until the cameraman was satisfied. Years later I learned that he wanted to capture the scene as part of a propaganda movie showing the world how the Soviet army had rescued Jewish children from the fascists.

At last, for the final time, Miriam and I, hand in hand, walked out of the barracks in matching striped uniforms. Miriam and I had survived Auschwitz. We were eleven years old.

Now we had only one question: How exactly would we get home?

CHAPTER ELEVEN

All around us people were preparing to leave. They just walked away from camp. I did not know what direction to take. I had no idea where on earth we were. I did not know there were countries called Poland and the Soviet Union. Having gone to school in a small village in Romania, I had learned nothing about the rest of the world.

For the next two weeks, Miriam and I stayed in Auschwitz with many other former prisoners. At first we did not have enough to eat. I went back to the basement and filled my scarf with flour.

"*Nyet! Nyet!*" No! No! shouted a Soviet soldier. He fired a shot.

Frightened, I spilled the flour, ran outside, and raced back to Miriam. Later I realized that the soldier was not shooting at me the way the Nazis had. He was trying to scare me. The Soviets had taken charge of the camp and were trying to maintain order.

I do not remember organizing any food after that. The Soviets fed us soup with beans in it that tasted good. As soon

as Miriam and I started eating, we could not stop. By then
we knew that eating too much was bad for us, so Miriam
and I monitored each other. We did not want to die from
overeating like other twins we had known.

About four weeks later, we finally left Auschwitz. We
were taken in a horse and wagon to an orphanage in a monastery in Katowice, Poland. Later we found out that the arrangements had been made by the Soviets, who were working with the Red Cross and Jewish Refugee Organizations.
They tried to reconnect people or redirect them to wherever
they wanted to go.

When we arrived at the monastery, we were taken to our
new living quarters. I was shocked. Miriam and I were given
our own nice room. There were two beds with clean, white
sheets. Sheets! I had not seen a white sheet in almost a year.
I felt strange and out of place. No one had bothered to give
us baths; we were filthy and covered with lice. There was no
way I could sleep on that clean, white bed.

For a long time, I stared at the sheets. That night I ripped
them off the bed and went to sleep on the bare mattress. I
did not want to make everything dirty. It seemed wrong.

The nuns had also put beautiful toys in our room, but
the toys made me angry. Toys were for children, but my
childhood had ended on the selection platform. At Auschwitz, I could focus on only one thing: to keep myself and
Miriam alive. I was eleven years old, but I no longer knew
how to play. What I wanted and needed was warmth and
loving care.

16. *Two front children are Eva (left) and Miriam (right).*

17. Eva and Miriam as high school students in Cluj.

*18. The Csengeri family after the war. The parents, Zvi and
Rosie, are in the middle. The twins, Yehudit and Lea, are on
either side, and son Michael is being held by Zvi.*

19. *Eva milking a cow.*

20. *Top row (l to r): Eva, Mickey Kor, Mickey's niece Miri,
brother Shlomo, and sister-in-law Sara. In front is Mickey's
nephew AuShalom.*

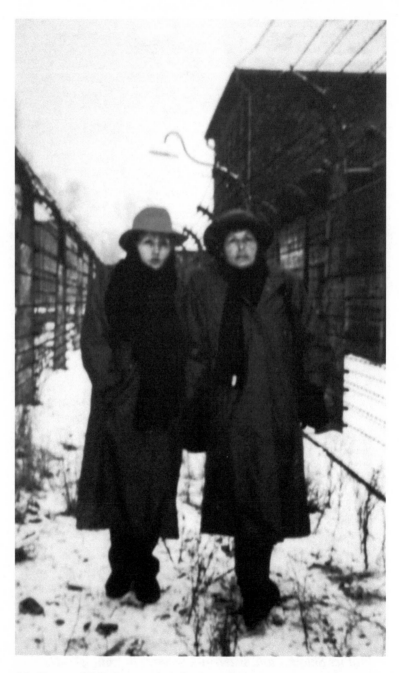

21. Eva and Miriam at Auschwitz, 1991.

22. *From middle left, Rina Kor (holding document), Alex Kor, Eva Mozes Kor, and Dr. Münch at Auschwitz in 1993 signing their statements.*

23. *Eva holding unused vials of substances used in experiments. The content of the vials is unknown; they have never been opened or tested.*

I became obsessed with the idea of going home. After all, I was free, wasn't I? I couldn't understand what the delay was. I have always been impatient and was especially impatient then. Why did it take so long?

One has to appreciate the situation facing the Soviets. They had found all these miserable souls and were confronted with the problem of trying to find out what to do with them. The war was still going on and they could not send us home. They asked questions and tried to find out where we wanted to go. I only wanted to go home. The Soviets considered us orphans, and we were, but we did not know or want to believe that at the time.

I spoke up for Miriam and me. "We're twins. That's Miriam, and I am Eva Mozes. Our father is Alexander and our mother is Jaffa. We are from Portz." We spoke to them in Hungarian because we did not speak Polish; a translator then told them what we had said. Conversations took a long time.

"Where are your parents?" asked the nuns.

"I don't know."

"Who will take care of you?"

"I don't know. We want to go home," I kept telling them.

They said, "Children cannot be released if they do not have parents."

"But we do have parents," I said.

"Where?"

"I have to go home to find out if they came back from the camp," I said. Now that we were safe, I could still hope to find Mama and Papa and my sisters.

They told us we could not leave unless there was someone to take care of us. I could not convince them there would be someone there. So there we had to stay. I began to wonder whether we were really free.

I felt extremely uncomfortable living in a Catholic monastery. Crosses, crucifixes, and paintings of the Virgin and Child surrounded us and seemed foreign. I longed for someplace more familiar. I wondered what my papa, a religious Jew, would think if he saw Miriam and me in a monastery. The nuns did not try to convert us or anything like that, but it was just so strange a place to find ourselves.

Older girls who had survived Auschwitz and were staying at the monastery told us that we could go into the town of Katowice and ride the streetcar without paying for tickets. All we had to do was show the numbers tattooed on our arms. They told us we did not have to speak Polish or say anything. Since we spoke mainly Hungarian, that was a small relief.

So we went into town and found what they told us was true: we could ride the streetcars for free. Over and over, Miriam and I rode the streetcar from one end of town to the other. The sheer joy of being free, feeling the wind in our ears, and being able to choose what we did was so liberating to us.

Through the older girls, we learned that some survivors of Auschwitz were being held in a displaced persons (DO) camp at Katowice, including our friend from home, Mrs. Csengeri, and her twin daughters. One day I thought of a plan to get us out of the monastery.

"Come on, Miriam," I said. "We're going to see Mrs. Csengeri."

"Why?" asked Miriam.

"Just come with me."

We hopped on a streetcar and went to the camp. When we found Mrs. Csengeri, I began talking a mile a minute. "You were my mama's friend," I said. "We don't want to stay in the monastery, but they won't let us leave because we can't find our parents."

"Yes, I know," she replied. "But why are you telling me all this?"

I hesitated for a second and then blurted, "Would you sign a paper saying you are our aunt and get us out so we can go home?"

At first, Mrs. Csengeri said nothing. I am sure she was full of worry about her own family, her children's health, about her own safety. To take on two more girls was a big commitment. Finally she turned to us and slowly said, "Yes. Yes, I will. I will go to the monastery with you and sign the papers." She paused and then added, "And I will take you home with me."

I was overjoyed. I never thanked her for what she did, but I will never forget what she did or what it meant to Miriam and me.

In March of 1945 Miriam and I moved into the camp with Mrs. Csengeri and her daughters. The camp buildings were barracks, where most people were staying in large rooms with a number of other people. But Mrs. Csengeri managed to get a small, separate room for herself, her two daughters, us, and a lady, Mrs. Goldenthal, and her three children.

Mrs. Goldenthal's twin boys, Alex and Erno, were our age, and I discovered that they were selected at Auschwitz for Mengele's experiments like us. Mrs. Goldenthal stayed with them, and I found out later that she had hidden a younger child, Margarita, underneath her long skirt. She came into the camp with the child hidden in her dress. During her entire stay there, even in the Nazi barracks where she had kept Margarita under the mattress during inspections, she and the other women helped to conceal her child. Mrs. Goldenthal was also in the liberation pictures, carrying her little girl.

Now Mrs. Goldenthal and Mrs. Csengeri took care of all of us. They washed us, boiled our clothes, and got rid of the lice. Mrs. Csengeri sewed dresses for Miriam and me out of big Soviet khaki tunics and even fixed special food for us. Wearing those dresses and eating the food made Miriam and me feel like little girls again, almost like we were part of a family, being cared for by adults, the way it used to be.

The Soviet soldiers in charge of the camp gave us bread and a half a ruble every week to spend on anything we wanted. We had only to show our numbers to the Russian guards to leave the camp, so we would go to the open air market in Katowice. There was not a great deal at the market because the war was still going on, but people were trying to sell any extra items they had. Miriam and I went to buy an apple. In the camp we were given plain food that filled us, such as bread, potato soup, and meat. An apple was a luxury that we were thrilled to have.

One morning, after about six weeks, Mrs. Csengeri woke me up from a deep sleep. "Pack everything," she said, "because we're moving." We gathered our things together. Miriam and I, hand in hand in our matching khaki dresses, boarded a train with our small group. I had no idea where we were going, but we knew where we wished to go. All I wanted was to find my parents or somebody from my real family. All I wanted was to go home.

Chapter Twelve

Soviet soldiers took charge as Miriam and I began the journey home with Mrs. Csengeri, Mrs. Goldenthal, and their children. Although we rode in a cattle car, it was very different from our ride to Auschwitz. The train was not crowded, and there were built-in bunk beds with little mattresses that were comfortable. We loved to sit on the top bunk bed and look out the windows, which this time were not covered by barbed wire. At night we had as many blankets as we wanted. Miriam and I cuddled. We still did not talk about how we felt or what was going on, we just snuggled.

In the daytime, the doors of the train cars were left open. Often Miriam and I sat in the doorway with our legs dangling out. The train lumbered on the tracks so slowly you could almost run alongside. The wind brushed our faces, and the fresh air felt wonderful. We enjoyed watching fields and hills slide by. It was spring. Flowers bloomed, birds chirped.

We were no longer in danger. We were free.

Sometimes the train stopped for five or six hours. We'd get off, and Mrs. Csengeri would set up two bricks, make a small fire, and cook something in a pot. The Soviets gave us bread and rations, but we also took along some food. I no longer had to worry about feeding us. Mrs. Csengeri took over and never complained. When the conductor called that the train was about to leave, we hopped on again.

We were getting closer to Romania. On the train we sang and talked. Mrs. Csengeri and Mrs. Goldenthal said they were going to save the striped prison uniforms they had worn at Auschwitz and testify to the world what had happened there. "I'll tell my story," Mrs. Csengeri kept saying. "I will tell the world what these monsters did to us."

Back then I did not understand why that was so important. I could not imagine who would want to hear about Auschwitz, but the women kept discussing it. The question came up as to whether their husbands had survived. I wondered if anybody in my family had survived besides Miriam and me. Nobody really knew.

Sometimes we passed through villages and towns that had been destroyed by bombing. Brick buildings lay in ruins. Rubble covered the ground. Some places seemed altogether abandoned. We went from Katowice in Poland to Czernowitz near the Romanian border. At the outer edge of the city we stayed at a camp that may have been a labor camp or ghetto. The camp was similar to Katowice. We could go into town to buy something or walk through the village and no one would bother us. I loved to go outside the camp and explore.

One day I came to a hill that was unusually shaped. I picked flowers and gave them to Mrs. Csengeri, and she asked where I had found them. When I told her, she scolded me and said, "Don't you ever go there again. Hundreds and thousands of Jews were killed and buried there by the Nazis." I was stunned. I realized then that Jews had not just died in Auschwitz. They were murdered even in the Nazi-occupied Soviet Union.

We stayed at Czernowitz about two months, and then one afternoon we were told to pack up, and we were loaded into another cattle car with bunk beds. As the train rumbled on, the grownups realized that we should have already reached Romania; Transylvania had become part of Romania again—it was no longer Hungary. Mrs. Csengeri watched the signs and said we were going deeper into the Soviet Union. When the train crawled uphill, some people jumped off and rolled away from the tracks. "Where are they going?" I wondered.

For years I wondered what happened to them. Later I realized that many people were frightened of the Soviet Union and did not want to live under Communist rule.

After a week, we arrived at a refugee camp in Slutz. It was close to Minsk in the Soviet Union. We lived there for a couple of months with former prisoners from all over Europe. Finally, we were grouped according to our home countries.

One day in late September, we started back into Romania. Our first stop was Nagy Várad Oradea, Mrs. Goldenthal's town. She and her children went home. I was so envious—I wanted to be back in our home.

That night the rest of us stayed in a hotel near the train station and had dinner there. The food was very, very good, consisting of baked potatoes and fried eggs with seasoning, with apples and ice cream for dessert. For once, we were full after we ate. A Jewish agency gave us the money to pay our bill. Every town that once had a Jewish population now had a Jewish agency to take care of displaced persons like us and help reunite families.

The next day we boarded another train and rode south to Şimleu Silvaniei, Mrs. Csengeri's town, and she invited us to stay overnight. In the morning, we thanked her for taking care of us and took the first train to Portz, our village.

When the train stopped and the conductor called, "Portz!" I immediately recognized the station. Holding hands, Miriam and I got off at the top of the hill and started down to the village. "Let's go home," I said. I had to see it. I am not sure what I expected to find. Would everything be the way we had left it, only maybe a little disheveled from the months we had been away? In my mind, home meant Miriam and me, our sisters and my parents, the farm and our animals. Any homecoming had to include at least some of these, right? I allowed myself to hope that there would be something good waiting for us.

Hand in hand, Miriam and I walked through the village. We were wearing our matching Soviet khaki tunic dresses, and I still had the shoes from the camp, twice the size of my feet. When I took a step, the front of the shoe flopped down first. People came out of their houses and whispered to each other. Nobody spoke to us directly. They just stared at us as we walked down the street. Miriam and I still looked alike, and I had a feeling that the villagers knew who we were.

As we approached our house, my heart beat so hard I could hear it thumping. I could not wait to reach the gate. Finally—we would be home again! My memories of the house were of nice things and good times: warm beds and clothes that fit, a mother who cooked for us, a father who provided. My family.

But none of that was left when we returned to our property. Nothing but the untilled land and the bare walls of an empty house.

Everything looked neglected. Abandoned. I realized immediately that Papa and Mama had not returned. They would never have let the weeds grow so high. They would never have let the house become run down.

That was the moment we knew, Miriam and I, that we were all that were left of the Mozes family. Grandma and Grandpa Hersh—our mother's primary reason for not escaping to Palestine—were also gone. There was nobody else.

Still holding hands, Miriam and I went inside. We were surprised when Mama's dog Lily, a little red dachshund, ran out to greet us, barking and wagging her tail. All this time and there she was! She seemed to recognize us, and when we reached out to pet her, she licked our hands. I guess Jewish dogs were not taken to concentration camps, only Jewish people.

The house was dirty—and empty. Everything had been

taken. Furniture, curtains, dishes, linens, candlesticks—everything. I walked from room to room searching for any reminders, any remnants of the life I had once lived. I only found three crumpled photographs wadded up on the floor. I picked them up and saved them.

One picture showed my older sisters, Edit and Aliz, with three of our cousins. Another was of Edit, Aliz, Miriam, and me and our teachers back in 1942. The third photo was the last picture of my whole family, taken in the fall of 1943. In the black and white photo, Miriam and I were wearing our matching burgundy dresses. This was the only proof I had that once, not so long ago, I had a family.

Miriam and I stayed for six or seven hours, roaming around the farm. The fruit trees were still there, and we ate some plums and apples, but villagers had picked most of the fruit.

By midafternoon our cousin Shmilu showed up. Aunt Irena, our father's youngest sister, had apparently sent word to him to come and get us. We later found out that she traced us through the Red Cross. Miriam and I were among the last Jews to return to Transylvania, and Aunt Irena had continued to check lists to see if anyone from our family had survived. Thus she knew exactly when our train was due to arrive in Portz and had contacted Shmilu.

Shmilu was about twenty years old and had lived in a nearby village. He, too, had been imprisoned at Auschwitz and was the only one of his immediate family to survive. I told him the neighbors had stolen everything. "Yes," he said,

"I know." The empty house was one more sign that no one had cared about us, and I harbored ill feeling toward the villagers for years.

In 2014, when I returned to Romania, I was warmly welcomed. The older villagers who were alive when we were taken away said they assumed our family would never return. They had all heard about death camps, and from their viewpoint, when Jews were taken by the Nazis, they did not come back. The villagers were poor, so they had taken things they could use.

Shmilu had gone to the neighbors and reclaimed a bed, a table, and a couple of chairs to fix up a room for himself in the summer kitchen of our farm. He was working the land and taking care of Lily. The dog wandered in and out, eating scraps around the farms.

We asked Shmilu questions about our parents. "I have not seen anyone from your family," he told us. "I know only that your Aunt Irena survived and is waiting for you." She had been sent to a concentration camp but had returned in May.

I did not feel comfortable in the house even though it was ours. I did not feel as though I belonged there anymore. Miriam and I had no home, no parents, no sisters. But we still had each other.

We left with Cousin Shmilu. Villagers stood at their gates and silently watched us go. I was angry with them but said nothing. We boarded a train that would take Miriam and me to the big city of Cluj to join our aunt.

Somehow, we would make a new life for ourselves.

CHAPTER THIRTEEN

For the next five years, from 1945 to 1950, Miriam and I lived with Aunt Irena. She owned a large apartment house in Cluj.

Aunt Irena was among the very few aunts that we knew very well. She was the youngest girl in my father's family and was very close to my father. Before the war, Miriam and I always enjoyed visits to Aunt Irena's home and her visits to see us. She would usually come in her chauffeur-driven car with her son, Laci, who was a young, handsome attorney and our favorite cousin. He would always play games with us and let us win. Aunt Irena and her husband traveled extensively, and she would tell us stories of vacations on the French Riviera and Monte Carlo. We loved to see her jewelry and furs.

But over the next year or two after our arrival in Cluj, we discovered that freedom was not what we had thought it would be. Life was not going back to the way it had been before the war. Romania was now controlled by the Communist Party, the only political party in the country, and with complete power in every area of life. The secret police force arrested anyone opposed to the government and took over people's property and gave it to the peasants.

During the war, the Nazis had forced Aunt Irena to work in a bomb factory in Germany. Her husband and son had perished in the camps. When she returned to Cluj, she found that the Communists had taken most of her possessions. However, the State let Aunt Irena keep her building because she was a war widow and a survivor of the concentration camps. She married a pharmacist who was also a survivor.

We all lived together, but we were not really a family. We knew our aunt cared about us because she was the only one of our relatives willing to take us in. But Aunt Irena never hugged or kissed us, or spoke to us with warmth or kindness after the war. I am sure she was trying to overcome her own issues, while she was dealing with two eleven-year-old girls who had returned from the barracks of Auschwitz with health and emotional problems. But above all, Miriam and I hungered for affection and yearned for a loving mother. Aunt Irena still had Persian rugs, a porcelain collection, and some designer clothes left from her prewar days. These treasures reminded her of the good life she used to have and seemed to mean more to her than we did.

Miriam and I felt out of place in that grand apartment. We were sloppy and messy. We did not belong in Auschwitz, but we did not entirely belong in this fancy apartment in Cluj, either.

Every night I had nightmares. I dreamed of rats the size of cats, dead bodies, and needles stuck into me. We heard the rumor that the Nazis had made soap out of Jewish fat, and I dreamed that soap bars spoke to me in the voices of my parents and sisters, asking me, "Why are you washing with us?" I did not tell Miriam because I was afraid I would make her feel bad and give her nightmares, too.

We both developed more health problems and caught colds all the time. Painful sores covered our bodies; some were as big as apples and formed scars. When Aunt Irena took us to the doctor, I was terrified—I remembered Dr. Mengele and his assistants in white coats. I had learned not to trust doctors so much.

When the Romanian doctor examined us, he said, "These children have what many war children are suffering from: malnutrition. There is nothing wrong with them that vitamins and a good diet cannot fix."

Our aunt tried to get us vitamins, but they were not available, and food was scarce. We stood in line for hours to get a loaf of bread, but after five or six hours we would reach the front of the line only to be told there was no more bread. Very few commodities were available for the public to buy. As a result, we frequently ate at a nearby orphanage.

Our aunt hired our cousin to run my father's farm and grow food for us. Cousin Shmilu brought flour, potatoes, eggs, vegetables, and sunflower oil, all from the farm. Miriam and I craved that oil and drank it straight from the bottle. This worried Aunt Irena, but the doctor told her to let us drink it, that we seemed to be getting better.

One day as I was eating white bread on the veranda of the apartment, someone saw me and reported me to the secret police. That night the police came and raided the apartment and seized all our food. They told us we were "sabotaging the system," and we could not have anything but what our rations allowed. The next day my aunt built a fake cabinet that looked like a wall. You could only get in there by pushing a button. From then on, we hid our food in the cabinet.

One night the secret police picked up Aunt Irena's husband without any explanation. He disappeared, and we did not know whether he was alive or dead. When we walked outside, we always worried about who was watching or listening. Someone could turn us in to the secret police.

Life in communist Romania became more and more difficult. The government controlled everything, including schools. On the first day of high school, Miriam and I wore our matching khaki dresses. We remembered going to school in Portz in our matching burgundy dresses. Now all the children made fun of us because of our clothes. We had only missed a year and a half of school and were not far behind in our studies. School, however, was harder for us because we spoke Hungarian, and classes were taught in Romanian.

At school we were the only Jews. Other students called us names despite what we had been through. Antisemitic people in Cluj spread rumors that at night a Jewish vampire stalked Christian girls and sucked their blood. When

Miriam and I were walking home from the orphanage in the evenings after our meal, I kept thinking, how will this vampire know I am Jewish and not attack me?

Even though we had been liberated from the camps, we did not feel free under the communist rule, and we were still suffering for being Jewish. But it was not just the Jews who were being persecuted. Conditions were terrible for everyone. Eventually, Miriam and I went to a Jewish Zionist organization to learn about Palestine, but the government later shut the organization down.

Sometimes we received packages from our aunt in the United States. Once she sent some fabric, and Aunt Irena took us to the seamstress and had three sets of matching dresses made for Miriam and me. Our favorite was blue with little polka dots. We loved wearing matching dresses to attract attention and fool the boys. Our American aunt also sent coats, but they were adult styles and did not fit.

One day in 1948, when we were fourteen, the government announced that a store would have new coats for sale. Miriam and I stood in line all night waiting for the store to open at ten o'clock in the morning. But twelve thousand people showed up—for two hundred coats! When the doors opened and people rushed in, a saleslady who was a friend of our aunt recognized us. She threw us two coats and shoved us under a counter. When the crowd subsided, we paid for them and walked out with matching rust-colored coats, the color of autumn leaves. We were still wearing those coats when we sailed to Israel years later.

Palestine became the state of Israel in 1948. I began to think it would be a privilege to live in a place where my father had dreamed of living. The last time we saw Papa, he made us promise that if we survived, we would go to Palestine.

Miriam and I exchanged letters with Uncle Aaron, our Papa's brother, who lived in Haifa, and we sent him a picture of us. Uncle Aaron offered to help us resettle and ease our suffering. We wrote him and asked if there was chocolate in Israel. He replied, telling us that we could eat all the chocolate we wanted and all the oranges we wanted, too. He would take care of us. We thought Israel sounded like paradise.

Aunt Irena told us she received news that her son was alive and living in Israel, and she wanted to emigrate, too. We all applied for exit visas, and our aunt's was granted easily. It took Miriam and me two years to obtain ours. The government did not want to let young people leave Romania because they needed the youth to rebuild the war-ravaged country.

Nevertheless we started preparing for our trip. The rules changed daily about what we could take. We packed a year before we left and lived surrounded by boxes filled with things we wanted to take. In order to leave the country, Miriam and I had to sign over our remaining property. The Communists had already claimed most of the farm to divide among the peasants, but we still owned two acres of farmland and the house in Portz. We wanted to leave so badly, we signed it over.

Two months before we left Romania, Aunt Irena's husband was released from prison and given a visa. He did not say a word to us girls about what had happened to him. We did not ask questions; we were just glad he had been freed.

Finally in June 1950, when we were about to leave, the government informed us that all we could take was what we could wear. The day we left, Aunt Irena had us put on three dresses underneath our matching coats. I carefully wrapped the creased photos of my family in paper and brought them with me.

We took a train to Constanza, a port on the coast of the Black Sea. Pushing and shoving, we lined up to board the ship, the Transylvania, one of the last three ships to leave before Romania's borders were closed for ten years. Miriam and I were squashed, and I could hardly breathe, but we tightly clutched each other's hands so we would not be separated. There were three thousand people on a ship built to hold only a thousand, and we stayed on deck for the entire voyage because there were not enough rooms for us all. We waited for twenty-four hours before we set sail.

As we pulled away from shore, I felt no sadness. I knew there was nothing left for Miriam and me in Romania. During the past five years, I had continued to hope that our sisters or parents might come back. The Jewish organizations working with the Red Cross had posted lists of people returning. Every night I checked the lists at the orphanage where we ate dinner, but there was no sign of any member of my family. Miriam and I were sixteen years old. We needed to move on.

It was a long, tiring trip. For days and days, we saw no land, but it was exciting to be on the open sea. The endless stretch of water and sky, fresh air, and the wind sifting through our hair smelled of freedom and promise. Hand in hand, Miriam and I watched dolphins jumping in and out of the ocean.

Early one morning our ship approached Haifa. As the boat docked, we stood on the deck and watched the sun rise over Mount Carmel, Israel. It was one of the most beautiful sights I had ever seen: the land of freedom. Most of the passengers on the ship were Holocaust survivors like us, and everyone burst into the Israeli national anthem, "Hatikvah." We were crying and singing with joy.

As we disembarked at the port, we searched for a person searching for us. Uncle Aaron finally spotted us, yelling our names and waving his arms so we would be sure to see him. I remember thinking how much he looked like my father. We hugged, and he kissed us. We cried in his arms. It had been so long since my sister and I had received any real affection from anyone besides each other.

My twin sister and I, in our matching rust-colored coats and layers of matching dresses, felt at last that we had come home.

CHAPTER FOURTEEN

When we arrived in Haifa with Uncle Aaron, we learned that Aunt Irena's son was not there after all. She had made up the story to get a visa. Miriam and I were sad to realize that our favorite cousin was actually gone forever.

We spent the afternoon with Uncle Aaron and his family. We met my cousin and her children for the first time. As newcomers, however, we were not allowed to stay with my uncle yet. It was only because my uncle transported immigrants from the port to the immigration center, he was able to sneak us out for the day. He wanted to see us and have us meet the rest of the family.

We were all sent to immigration centers. Aunt Irena and her husband went to one, and Miriam and I went to another. We were processed into the country and then sent to a children's village for the initial six weeks of quarantine. We were given all kinds of shots and Israeli clothes, including shorts, which were new to us.

When the quarantine period was over, Miriam and I were sent to one of the Youth Aliyah Villages, agricultural centers set up by the Israeli government. We were happy that we would live with other children and did not have to stay with our aunt. Our village was set up to make a newcomer feel accepted into the community, regardless of age. Upon our arrival, we were put into groups and would become friends. Each dormitory had a housemother, but we would take care of our own rooms. Two girls were assigned to Miriam and me as "big sisters" and made us feel at home.

The villages were located on huge farms where young people like us planted and harvested crops and tended the animals. At our village, we worked half the day and went to school half the day. My jobs were to milk cows and pick tomatoes and peanuts.

Miriam and I were at the village with about three hundred other teenagers from many different countries. Not all of the youth were Holocaust survivors or orphans. Some lived at the village while their parents trained for jobs. The food we produced helped feed the new nation of Israel with a growing population.

For the first time since leaving Auschwitz, I would sleep without having nightmares. I would no longer have to worry about our physical safety or survival. No one would call me a "dirty Jew." Instead, we were not just allowed but encouraged to celebrate our Jewish heritage. Our hurts and suffering would slowly begin to heal in those youth villages.

Although we all arrived speaking a variety of languages, we were taught a common language: Hebrew. I learned a few words the very first night Miriam and I spent at the village, a Friday. That night and every Friday night, all the kids gathered in a huge dining room to welcome the *Shabbat*, the Jewish Sabbath. We all wore white shirts, and there were candles and wine on the tables.

After prayers, everyone started singing and dancing the *hora*. But I did not know how. "Can I do this dance?" I wondered. My big sister took my hand, Miriam's big sister grasped hers, as everyone joined hands and formed a circle. We danced to the right. I did not know the steps but I followed along. With arms raised high, we danced together, boys and girls, all of us singing "Hava Nagila." Laughing, we danced round and round, faster and faster. I danced the *hora* and was filled with joy. Miriam and I were finally part of a new, large, welcoming family.

Eva's Epilogue

In Israel we lived for two years in the Youth Village. We went to school half the day and worked on the farm for the other half. We learned Hebrew quickly, within two years rapidly skipping up from one class to the next, finally finishing in the tenth grade. Miriam worked in the field, and I was a milkmaid. I was the only girl working with six guys. I learned to say "I love you" in ten different languages, which, at age sixteen, seemed like an important thing to know.

I wish all children who have been through severe trauma and in need of a healing environment could live in a similar home. There is something soothing, healing about helping plants grow and taking care of animals. Israel had many traumatized children coming into the country, and with the help of psychologists, they understood what we needed and how to set up a system to provide for those needs. Many children and youth in the world could benefit from similar systems.

In 1952 we were drafted into the Israeli army, where Miriam studied nursing and became a registered nurse. I studied drafting and became a draftswoman, drawing plans of buildings or machines. I was stationed in Tel Aviv and stayed in the Israeli Army for eight years, reaching the rank of sergeant major. Those years were growing years for me. I became a very good draftswoman and I learned that I was able to earn a living and support myself, but I felt I didn't belong anywhere. On holidays I would occasionally stay with relatives, but I felt I was a guest, not a real family member, so I tried to clean, wash the dishes, and be of some help. Sometimes I preferred to stay in an army hotel alone. But I longed for a home of my own.

In 1960, I was living a pretty good life in Israel. By then I earned good money and lived in an apartment in Tel Aviv. In April of that year, I met an American tourist, Michael Kor, who was visiting his brother and family in Tel Aviv. He was also a Holocaust survivor; he spent four years in Buchenwald and Magdaberg. Even though we didn't speak the same language—he spoke English and I spoke Hebrew—we were both looking for someone to share a life with, creating a home and family. His brother and family liked me, and that was important, because I wanted to be part of a large, loving family again.

During one meeting, he said something to me in English that I didn't understand but seemed important. That night I looked it up and replied, "Yes." It was a marriage proposal. Though we could hardly communicate, we were wed a few weeks later.

The next thing I knew, I was a married woman living in Terre Haute, Indiana, where my husband Michael, now known as Mickey, had lived since 1947. He had come to Terre Haute after the war specifically to live close to his liberator, Col. Andrew Nehf from the U.S. Allied Forces, who sponsored his immigration to the U.S. and was always a friend to our family.

I can tell you that it is not a particularly good idea to marry someone without being able to communicate in the same language. Both of us had too many surprises to contend with while getting to know one another. For instance, he initially thought I was a very quiet person. As you might have figured out from this memoir, I am not; I seemed quiet because I could not speak any English.

Coming from Tel Aviv to Terre Haute was like landing on the moon. I knew nothing about life in the U.S., spoke no English, and thought everyone was rich. Within a few weeks, I was pregnant. I was very homesick, missing Miriam and my friends in Israel, and I watched TV to drown out my loneliness. At the time, I thought that American shows on television were all news and sports, because those were the only two kinds of programs that my husband watched.

One day, to my surprise, there was a TV show (what I later learned Americans called "soap operas") about a young couple dating, kissing, and living like young people do. Now this was a show worth watching! I became engrossed, looking away from the action only to jot down words I did not know so I could later look them up in the dictionary. I then proceeded to memorize those words. When I repeated the words I learned to Mickey, he asked, "What in the world are you watching?' In this way I learned to speak English well enough to get a job within three months of my arrival to the States.

Our son, Alex Kor, was born in 1961, and our daughter, Rina Kor, in 1963. I thought my life was complete, but my childhood experiences continued to haunt me. The birthday parties started, which became a problem because my children asked me why they had no grandparents like all their friends did.

When Alex was six years old and a very popular kid, his friends came over to play tricks on him. Those tricks reminded me of the days when the Nazi youth harassed us in Portz, days when I was helpless and could do nothing to defend myself.

But this time I lived in this great country where I did not have to put up with it. I went outside and chased those kids away. Because of this I became very "popular" with the kids at Halloween. Every year the harassment would begin on October 1st. They painted swastikas on our home and put white crosses in the yard—it was awful.

Alex would come home from school crying and saying, "Mom, I'm so ashamed of you! All the kids say that you are crazy! Why can't you be like all the other mothers?" I told my son that I was not crazy, but neither was I like all the other mothers. I thought that if I could tell the story of what had happened to me as a child, the kids would understand and leave me alone to live in peace in my home. But as a victim of such atrocities, I did not know how to accomplish this.

I was harassed for eleven years until 1978, when NBC

aired the show "Holocaust." Suddenly everybody understood why I was different. Those same kids who had taunted me at Halloween called me or wrote to me to apologize.

I began lecturing in 1978, invited by schools and other groups, and people always asked me about the details of the experiments. I never knew all the details about Auschwitz, but I thought that there would be lots of information available about the camps and about Dr. Mengele. Unfortunately, I could not find any information in any book. Very little had been written, and the medical records of the experiments were taken by Mengele. I remembered that in the liberation film, about two hundred children were shown marching out of the camp. If I could contact those children, now adults, we could share our memories and piece together what had been done to us. But I didn't know where to find them.

It took me six years to come up with the idea of forming an organization to help me and Miriam locate the Mengele twins. In 1984 we founded CANDLES, an acronym for Children of Auschwitz Nazi Deadly Lab Experiments Survivors. We located 122 survivors living in ten countries and on four continents. CANDLES, as a support group, helped many twins deal with some of the special issues that we all had as survivors of Mengele's experiments.

As time went on, Miriam had more and more problems with her kidneys. We knew it had something to do with the injections she was given in Auschwitz, but we didn't know what she was injected with that kept her kidneys from growing beyond the size of a ten-year-old's. By 1987 her kidneys failed. I donated my left kidney, which helped her live until June 6, 1993. We never did find out what she or any of us had been injected with. I am still searching and hoping to discover this information.

Miriam's death was devastating to me. I knew that I had to do something positive in her memory. So in 1995 I opened the CANDLES Holocaust Museum and Education Center, in Terre Haute, Indiana. Over 140,000 people have visited the museum since we opened its doors, most of them young people.

In 1993, I had an unexpected life-changing event. I was invited by a doctor to speak at a medical ethics conference, and I accepted. Then the doctor asked, "Would it be possible to bring a Nazi doctor with you?" I said, "Well, I don't know where to find one of those. The last I checked, they weren't advertising in the Yellow pages."

After the conference, I remembered that ZDF, a public television broadcaster in Germany, had aired a documentary that included an interview with a former Nazi doctor named Münch, who worked in Auschwitz. I contacted ZDF, asking for contact information, thinking that he might know something about the twin experiments. ZDF not only gave me his contact information but helped to arrange a meeting between us. The doctor did not want to come to the U.S., but he agreed to meet with me at his home.

In spite of being the world's best sleeper and champion nap taker, I couldn't sleep the two nights before I was to fly to Germany.

While I badly wanted to learn more about the experiments and to hear more about a visit he had from the Mengele family, I was actually terrified of being in a room with him. My memories from Auschwitz when I was a guinea pig were nightmares I did not want to experience again. I also didn't know why this Nazi doctor would be willing to meet me. I had watched a previous interview of him in which he seemed very stiff, unpleasant—in general, a good old Nazi. It was hard to trust his motives, and it added to my nerves.

I packed feverishly, including my new outfit I bought just for that occasion because I wanted to look my best. I wanted no Nazi doctor to ever feel sorry for me. Still, I felt confused and very nervous.

On August 17, 1993, I flew to Amsterdam to meet my Dutch friend, resistance fighter, and translator Tony Van Renterghem, and his wife, Susan Severeid, along with a production crew from RTL television who were going to tape our meeting. We were flying to Munich and then driving from there to meet with Dr. Münch at his house.

There was so much stress no matter which way I turned. The RTL producers pressured me not to ask Dr. Münch questions that might upset him, because he could stop the interview. On the flight to Munich, RTL producers reviewed my list of questions and continued to pressure me to be polite and easy-going so I would not ask any serious questions.

I really did not need any of this added pressure, and I was determined to ask the doctor questions about our experiments and the Mengele family visit. I reasoned that if I asked about the experiments and Mengele at the end, then even if Dr. Münch stopped the interview, it would be at the end of our meeting and the producers would have gotten the interview they wanted. I had to learn as much as I could.

We arrived at his house, my heart beating fast, and we rang the doorbell. A gray-haired man with a gray goatee beard and a big smile opened the door and shook my hand. I said, "Dr. Münch, I am Eva Kor, and this is Susan Severeid." He spoke English and asked us in. He invited us to sit on the sofa in his living room, and then he introduced us to his daughter who was visiting from Canada. I was still nervous, but his handshake and big smile helped.

The producers and videographers did not like the light in the living room, so Dr. Münch suggested that we go to the back porch. As we were sitting on some outdoor metal chairs, the 82-year-old doctor went into his house five times and each time he returned with a big fluffy pillow that he handed me. After the fifth pillow, I asked him, "What are you doing?" He answered, "I want to make sure that you are comfortable sitting on this metal chair." I was stunned that a Nazi doctor was concerned about my comfort, surprised that he was so polite and kind.

It was a very nice sunny day, and on the horizon I could see the mountains of the Austrian border, peaceful and majestic. I pinched myself because, even more surprising than his kindness, was that I liked Dr. Münch, and I told him so. I said it was very strange that I, a survivor of Auschwitz, liked this Nazi doctor.

I asked him if he knew anything about the twin experiments. He said no, that the twin experiments were top secret, and only Dr. Mengele and people immediately under him knew anything about them.

Then, without any planning to do so, I spontaneously asked him if he knew anything about the gas chambers in Auschwitz. He said "This is the nightmare I live with every day of my life." I was shocked to hear that Nazis also had nightmares; I thought only survivors did.

He continued, telling me that he had refused to do the life-or-death selections at Auschwitz and was given a special permit to avoid it. He added that he did not want to decide who would live and who would die. I knew that for some reason, he was trying to impress me that he was a better person than most Nazis.

He went on to describe the gas chamber operations in detail, saying, "People would be told they were taking a shower after their journey and to remember their clothes hanger number and to tie their shoes together."

He said when the victims entered the shower room, they saw clean and polished floors, shining shower heads, and the scent of perfume filled the air, so they were looking forward to a nice warm and refreshing shower after the journey they had been through.

"When the gas chamber was fully packed, the doors closed hermetically and sealed. A vent-like orifice opened in the ceiling, dropping pellets like gravel to the floor. Somehow the pellets operated like dry ice and turned to gas, and the gas began rising from the floor.

"People tried to get away from the rising gas, climbing on top of one another. The strongest people ended atop a pile of intermingled bodies. When the people on the top of the pile stopped moving, that was when I knew, from looking through a peephole and watching it all, that everybody was dead." Dr. Münch said he signed the mass death certificates; there were no names on them, only that there were two thousand or three thousand dead people.

I told Dr. Münch that this was very important information, for I had not known that the gas chambers worked that way. I had read many books and watched many films, but the information he was providing me I had never read or heard. I felt this was unique information that I had to record and make public.

I asked him if he would come with me to Auschwitz in 1995, when we would be celebrating the fiftieth anniversary of our liberation from the camp. I also asked him if he would sign an affidavit about what he had said and seen and done, and to do it at the site of all those killings in front of witnesses. I wanted to have this affidavit for historic documentation of the gas chambers. I knew there were Holocaust deniers, and I thought maybe some who doubted the word of Jewish survivors would believe the word of a Nazi doctor. Dr. Münch immediately said that he would love to.

I would never have believed it would be that easy, but I was very pleased. And I had to wonder how this all happened, so many things that clicked into place. I was asked to speak at a conference and then to find a Nazi doctor. Not only did I find one, he was willing to meet me at his house. I had never thought ahead of time to ask about the gas chambers—it just seemed to pop out of my mouth. I thought about how amazing it was that the only Nazi I ever met after liberation from Auschwitz was actually stationed at the gas chambers. Not only that, he was willing to talk about it, and then beyond that, he was willing to document it. I was not a particularly religious person, but even I wondered how all this evolved so smoothly; it was as if someone was directing it.

I returned from Germany, and I was so happy that I would have an important, original document witnessed and signed by a Nazi—a participator, not a survivor or a liberator—to add to the historical collection of information we were preserving for ourselves and for future generations.

I felt so grateful to Dr. Münch, his willingness to come with me to Auschwitz and sign that document, and I wanted to thank him. But how can one thank a Nazi doctor? I visited a Hallmark card shop, but nothing there fit the occasion. What does one give a Nazi doctor? I wanted to give him something meaningful, but I couldn't think of anything that felt right.

For ten months, I constantly pondered this question. All kinds of ideas popped into my head but I dismissed them until I finally thought, how about a simple letter of forgiveness from me to him? Forgiving him for all that he has done?

I knew immediately that he would appreciate it, but what I discovered once I made the decision was that forgiveness is not so much for the perpetrator, but for the victim. I had the power to forgive. No one could give me this power, and no one could take it away. That made me feel powerful. And feeling like I had any power over my life as a survivor made me feel good. All those years I was angry and bitter, my feelings were still being controlled by the Nazis. When I let the anger go, I felt in control, a very good feeling.

I wrote and rewrote my letter to Dr. Münch for four months, working through a lot of pain. Concerned about my spelling, I called my former English professor, Susan Kaufman, to correct my letter. We met a few times, and then one day she said, "Eva, your problem isn't Dr. Münch. Your problem is Dr. Mengele." She asked me to think about forgiving Dr. Mengele, as well.

At first I was shocked by that suggestion, but at a later date, I promised her that I would, for I had realized that I even had the power to forgive the Angel of Death. "Wow," I thought. "It makes me feel good that I can do that. I have that power, and I am not hurting anyone with it." And then I decided I would forgive all the Nazis.

We arrived in Auschwitz on January 27, 1995. Dr. Münch came with his son, daughter, and granddaughter, and I came with my son, Alex, and my daughter, Rina. Dr. Münch signed his document. Then I read my own personal statement of forgiveness, and I signed it.

Immediately I felt that a burden of pain had been lifted from my shoulders, a pain I had lived with for fifty years. I was no longer a victim of Auschwitz, no longer a victim of my tragic past. I was free. I also took that moment to forgive my parents, whom I had hated all my life for not protecting us from Auschwitz, for not saving us from growing up as orphans. I finally understood that they had done the best that they could. I also forgave myself for hating my parents in the first place.

Anger and hate are seeds that germinate war. Forgiveness is a seed for peace. It is the ultimate act of self-healing. Forgiveness has nothing to do with the victimizers. It does not condone them, excuse them, or endorse them. No one asks to be a victim. Forgiveness is the only power a victim has to heal, liberate, and empower themself. I believe it is a human right to live free of pain.

If you have been a victim of something that still causes you pain, imagine how you would feel if it never happened to you? If you are thinking about forgiveness, begin by writing a letter to the person who hurt you, working through your pain, but **do not** send your letter. Forgiveness is only for you. Forgiveness does not mean reconciliation with the victim; it could be dangerous to be in contact with the person who hurt you. In fact, I believe people have to feel safe to forgive. No one can forgive on the battlefield. That is why forgiveness is a personal decision and can only be done when a person is in the circumstances, a place of safety, and mindset to do so.

Some readers might think writing a forgiveness letter sounds silly, that it would not help. I say to just try it. The only thing you can lose is your pain. And if you don't like the way you feel without the pain in your life, you can take it back and no one will stop you.

I look at forgiveness as the summit of a very tall mountain. One side is dark, dreary, wet, and very difficult to climb. But those who struggle up and reach the summit can see the beauty of the other side of the mountain, which is covered by flowers, white doves, butterflies, and sunshine. Standing at the summit we can see both sides of the mountain. How many people would choose to go back down on the dreary side rather than stroll through the sunny flower-covered side?

I have given over 3,000 speeches throughout the world, written two books, and been the subject of two documentaries, the most recent, *Eva-7063*, winning numerous awards. I hope to teach young people the life lessons I have learned through all my pain and everything I have been through and survived:

1. Never ever give up on yourself or your dreams, for everything good in life is possible.
2. Judge people on their actions and the content of their character.
3. Forgive your worst enemy and forgive everyone who has hurt you—it will heal your soul and set you free.

To young readers, I want to say: I know growing up is hard. But if I could survive the Nazis, you can survive the challenges you are facing. If I can forgive the Nazis, you can forgive whoever has hurt you and find happiness.

When I look back on my teenage years, I would never have believed that anyone would want to listen to me or that I would have anything important to say. But I am saying to you, whoever is reading this book, to remember: never ever give up. You can survive and make your dreams come true.

And I would like to end with a quote from my Declaration of Amnesty read at the fiftieth anniversary of the liberation of Auschwitz:

"I hope, in some small way, to send the world a message of forgiveness: a message of peace, a message of hope, a message of healing.

Let there be no more wars, no more experiments without informed consent, no more gas chambers, no more bombs, no more hatred, no more killing, no more Auschwitzes."

Afterword

Surviving the Angel of Death was published in 2009, and Lisa Rojany Buccieri captured Eva Kor's voice and story as Eva wanted it to be told. The first-person narrative provides insight into what Eva was thinking and feeling, but it doesn't necessarily convey what it was like to know Eva, the events in the last ten years of her life, and the stories behind the stories, both positive and negative.

Eva—and she always told everyone to call her Eva—was a tiny woman. At the end of her life, she was 4'9", but she stood out in any crowd, always decked out in her signature look: the Eva Kor blue pantsuit. She changed it up by wearing different scarves or a printed blouse topped with a blue vest, but it was always a particular bright blue. She said, "I am somebody because of who I am inside, and no outfit can change that. I do like to look good, and I like blue because I like the way it looks on me, and it makes it simpler to dress, like a uniform. I don't have to waste any more time and effort on it. I do not like to wear black, my topic is too dark, and I like to liven up my appearance."

If the book gives readers the impression that Eva could be stubborn, singled-minded, willing to do or say something people might not like, that was true to life. Those very qualities enabled Eva and Miriam's survival in Auschwitz. Eva acknowledged that her father's harshness prepared her for the camp; likewise, her parents' secrecy and denials made Eva realize that adults don't always tell the truth, making her less gullible to believe anything the Nazis said, which saved Eva and Miriam's lives more than once. As an adult, she was opinionated and direct, at times combative. But she always said, "Don't make me a saint. Don't put me on a pedestal. I don't want the pressure." To hear her speak, to hear her story and lessons, and to witness the magnitude of her generosity and her tireless efforts to help people from all walks of life, it was hard not to put her on a pedestal. But she was right to avoid sainthood. She showed us that it doesn't take a saint to forgive enemies, to be a champion, and to try to bring transformative peace and kindness to the world.

When Eva discovered the power of forgiveness to heal the decades of pain she had suffered from the Holocaust, the primary audience with whom she hoped to share her experience was other Holocaust survivors. Both before and after her forgiveness, she was a relentless advocate for survivors and Holocaust-related concerns. She was a catalyst in the movement to pressure governments worldwide to uncover and prosecute Nazi war criminals, responsible for millions of deaths, who were living freely, mostly in Europe or South America. She joined in the pursuit of financial justice for Holocaust survivors, and particularly for the Mengele twins. The twins received an apology from the Kaiser-Wilhelm Institute, and a lawsuit against Bayer was incorporated into a class action, which ended with a German settlement fund that made payments to survivors. She advocated for laws mandating Holocaust education in public schools, and she used her speaking fees to sponsor educators to go on her group trips to Auschwitz, so that they, in turn, could teach the Holocaust with more depth and insight. In a public statement on her forgiveness, Eva said, "Many people hold onto pain and anger. Unfortunately, this does not help the survivors, and that is my only focus. My forgiveness has nothing to do with the perpetrators. It is an act of self-healing, self-liberation, and self-empowerment. It's free, it has no side effects, and it works. I highly recommend that everyone try it."

Eva's forgiveness message was not universally well received, particularly in the beginning. Most survivors were offended, understandably, at hearing that Eva had forgiven the Nazis. It sounded to them like Eva had forgiven the Nazis on behalf of all survivors, when they did not want anyone to forgive the Nazis, much less on their behalf. It was an unfortunate misunderstanding, because from the day that Eva read her statement of amnesty at Auschwitz, saying, "I, Eva Mozes Kor, in my name only," she always stressed that forgiveness is a personal decision for individuals to make only for themselves, on their own timeline. She never meant for her forgiveness to be a blanket forgiveness on anyone's behalf but her own. Many survivors felt some things are simply too bad to forgive, and the Holocaust was in that category. It is not difficult to understand a view of the Holocaust as unforgivable; its existence testified to the outer limits of cruelty, greed, and hatred.

Another major factor that caused rejection of Eva's forgiveness lay in its definition; forgiveness was a word that Eva had redefined. Eva knew what she had done was not forgiveness in the traditional sense. Traditional forgiveness involves atonement and reconciliation between someone who has been hurt and the person who hurt them. There was no reconciliation or atonement found in Eva's forgiveness, and she considered justice a separate issue. She said, "I knew using the word 'forgiveness' in the way I was using it would cause confusion. I tried to think of another word, but no perfect term occurred to me. So I kept using the word 'forgiveness,' but I hoped I could explain to people what I meant and they would warm up to it." Unfortunately, that did not always happen. She often became frustrated with survivors who she felt were suffering needlessly, sometimes coming across as berating them or even criticizing them for not trying her forgiveness—unfairly, as her son, Alex, acknowledged. That also caused some to question her motivations.

One of the biggest moments of controversy surrounding Eva was when she traveled to Germany to attend the trial of Oskar Groening, known as the "accountant of Auschwitz." She had written a letter to Groening beforehand, in which she said:

"It is true, but sad, that we cannot change what happened in Auschwitz. I am hoping that you and I, as former adversaries, can meet as people who respect one another as human beings and can relate to one another to understand, to heal, and to express thoughts that would not be possible any other way. Any time adversaries meet to repair a relationship, they learn a great deal about themselves and how people function. It cannot be done on television, by telephone, or by Skype; it can only be done face to face.

"I am one of the Auschwitz survivors who has chosen to participate as a co-plaintiff in your case, and I am probably the only survivor who has forgiven all the Nazis, including you, in my name alone. My forgiveness does not absolve the perpetrators from taking responsibility for their actions, nor does it diminish my need and right to ask questions about what happened at Auschwitz."

Eva was aware that Groening had acknowledged his role in the Holocaust and expressed remorse. He had publicly spoken out on the activities in the camp, exposing the lies of Holocaust deniers as a personal witness to Nazi atrocities. Eva believed Groening deserved punishment, but felt that a sentence requiring him to speak about his experiences to students would contribute more to public good than sentencing him to jail. Eva felt that the trial should be more about healing of Nazi victims and prevention of neo-fascism.

At the end of the hearing's first day, Eva wanted to talk to Groening. When she arrived, he became emotional and tried to get up, but collapsed, sliding down from his wheel-chair. Eva grabbed his feet and her lawyer, Markus Gold-bach, held his upper body to stop his fall and avoid injury until the court marshals arrived to help.

Eva testified the next morning, reading her statement about her forgiveness and her thoughts on his punishment. At the lunch break, Eva approached Groening to shake his hand and tell him how important it was that he would speak the truth as he did in the past. As Goldbach described it: "In a spontaneous gesture, Groening pulled Eva slightly down and gave her a kiss on the cheek, overwhelmed with emotion. Eva was surprised but could not react, especially as she was so small. Eva and her lawyer both felt that he was not just grateful for Eva's ideas on his punishment but also moved by Eva's testimony of her suffering. Goldbach no-ticed that when Groening was testifying, he was switching between past and present, and it appeared that some part of him had never really left Auschwitz.

Groening's kiss became a photograph published by me-dia around the world, and it added to the image of Eva as a friend to Nazis. Articles about the trial and the photo in-cluded Eva's forgiveness, but rarely indicated that she had appeared to provide testimony that would help to convict Groening, and the stories did not attempt to clarify what Eva meant by forgiveness.

Groening and Eva's post-hearing kiss did indeed upset many survivors. For most people who read or watched the news stories, important context was lacking. Groening's actions after the war create a somewhat more understandable picture of Eva's acceptance of a spontaneous gesture of gratitude from a repentant, elderly man. Unfortunately for Eva, as with Dr. Hans Munch, Groening did not have any first-hand information on the medical experiments.

Eva's compassion extended to the people of Germany as well. During the writing of this book, she insisted that soldiers at Auschwitz not be referred to as German soldiers, but as Nazi soldiers. She knew that not all Germans were Nazis. She did not believe in inherited guilt and felt that to impose guilt on German people who were not even alive in WWII, much less involved in the Holocaust, was unfair. She shared a story:

"In 2005 I went to Germany with a friend, a German lady whose name is Gunda. I met Gunda in 2000 when she invited me to lecture at her school in Rockford, Illinois. She never liked to deal with WWII, nor the Holocaust. Since she was a little girl, she had been called a Nazi because she was German, but she was born after the war and knew nothing about the Nazis. She tried to stay as far away from the stories of the Holocaust as she could, but a teacher colleague encouraged her to invite me anyway. I was different, a survivor who had forgiven the Nazis.

"When I met Gunda, I told her that she didn't have to feel guilty for being born German, and she was only responsible for her own actions. We became very good friends, and she decided to go with me to Germany. I was the keynote speaker at a conference run by Albrecht and Brigitte Mahr.

"I had a great response after I spoke at the conference, and I was scheduled to conduct a three-hour workshop. Frankly, I was concerned what I could do with fifty people, to keep them busy and involved for three hours. As we were walking, a lady speaking English approached and introduced herself as Renee Levi, a child of a Holocaust survivor. She asked me if I knew any children of Nazis. I said, "Yes, Renee, meet Gunda." We ate lunch together, and they could not stop talking. There was a deep connection between those two.

"When I started my workshop, I thought that having Renee and Gunda share their stories and their emotional connection was an important way of showing how two children of former enemies connected. Then when I was readying to begin the workshop, ten people came up to me; they also wanted to share their thoughts. Then forty people came up to me to share their experiences and thoughts, and then three hours had passed, and that was the workshop.

"I learned that day the Germans carry a great deal of pain with them; four women had told of avoiding having babies because they did not want to have another generation of Germans feeling guilty for being Germans. The guilt and scars left on Germans for being German is difficult to understand, but it's there for many."

Eva was contacted by a German man, Michael Woerle, who was the grandson of Otmar von Verschuer, the mentor of Nazi Dr. Josef Mengele. Dr. Verschuer was with the Kaiser Wilhelm Institute where he developed and directed the twin experiments in Auschwitz. Verschuer's family had not known or acknowledged his work for the Nazis and his role in the Auschwitz experiments. After Woerle came across some of his grandfather's writings that he found disturbing, he researched more deeply. After his research led to the difficult truth, he reached out to Eva. They became fast friends, and Woerle accompanied Eva on her trips to Germany, helping with travel and meeting arrangements and acting as a guide and translator.

In 2014, on the annual trip to Auschwitz, the group with Eva noticed another group, made up of German high school girls, at the cattle car on the selection platform. Eva spotted the group and was told they were German. She approached them on the spot, as they were obviously distressed and emotional, with tears and red cheeks, and even more so when she told them she had been a prisoner there when she was ten years old. She then spoke to them kindly, giving each of them a hug, telling them, "You don't have to feel guilty. You didn't do this. You weren't even born. But what you do have is a responsibility to remember and share what you've seen. Be a witness, prevent this from ever happening again. Your duty is to go make the world a better place." The tour group watched the girls' tears turn into smiles, a special moment for everyone who witnessed it.

Eva was accused more than once of trying to start controversy in order to get attention. In general, it is almost impossible to avoid controversy when advocating for change, and Eva's redefinition of forgiveness was radical. While many felt that forgiveness should not occur without the victimizer

asking for forgiveness and offering atonement for that forgiveness, Eva always responded to this line of thought by
pointing out that requirement allows the victimizer to re-
tain control over the victim. Nazis were all dead or hiding,
or denying their role in the war. In her view, she or any other
survivor would be doomed to a life of anger and suffering if
they were required to wait for an apology that would never
come. Eva insisted that the right to be happy, to be free from
pain, should be viewed as a universal human right.

As for her desire for attention, when Eva did get the
spotlight, she used it as she always did, to educate people on
the Holocaust and the use of forgiveness to bring happiness
and peace to the world. Holding up two fingers in the clas-
sic peace sign became the signature Eva pose seen in many
photos, particularly near the end of her life.

Not all survivors felt alienated by Eva's actions. She had
friendships with a number of fellow survivors who did not
agree with her forgiveness but shared the bond of the Holocaust and their Jewish heritage, and respected her tireless work in Holocaust education. One survivor even found
the courage to return to Auschwitz for the first time in the
company of Eva. Many survivors of the Holocaust and other
genocides came to the museum in Terre Haute to speak.
For survivors in need, Eva was quick to provide emotional
and financial support. It's also worth noting that two of the
world's top Holocaust experts engaged with Eva. Rabbi Michael Berenbaum did not believe that Eva's forgiveness met
the requirements of Jewish law, but he respected her efforts

to provide Holocaust education. USC Shoah Foundation Director Stephen D. Smith chose to include Eva as one of the survivors in their Dimensions in Testimony program to share her Auschwitz experience and present her ideas of forgiveness, though he himself felt that determining who or what is forgivable to be a personal decision.

When Eva urged young people to "use their beautiful minds," another of her life lessons, she was drawing from her own past, when she sometimes took years to come up with solutions or answers that she needed. She never stopped thinking, she never stopped questioning, she never stopped her mental examination of life, of people, of her own story, of forgiveness, of humans in general—what motivates them and what helps them.

Eva's daily life was infused by her sense of mission, with a single-mindedness that is rare to find. Unless she had an engagement elsewhere, she showed up at her museum to lead tours, give talks to groups—especially the school groups. She also read all the emails she received, responding to questions, and giving advice, words of comfort, and words of encouragement to those who were struggling with issues in their own lives.

The best days were when she had school groups. Children and teens responded to Eva, because she spoke to them honestly, never speaking down to them. So often, adults think of childhood as a carefree period, but in fact, many children have unimaginably difficult lives, as Eva did herself. Eva also acknowledged that growing up is difficult, even in the best of circumstances. She spoke to kids and teens as intelligent human beings, with respect and understanding of the challenges in their lives, and they loved her for it. At her events, she made time for all who approached her.

One would think that a person who had been treated so cruelly by so many people in her life would be distrustful, would have a wall, a tough outer layer. But that was one of the contradictions of her character. She could be tough. She was a sergeant major in the Israeli army, and that sometimes became apparent. But she was amazingly open, and, with the exception of young people wearing distressed jeans—her pet peeve—she welcomed everyone into the museum, on her trips, and into her group of supporters.

Her list of life lessons continued to grow, beyond the basics listed in the epilogue. One of the last ones she added was "Be yourself, just be the best you that you can be."

Eva was true to her advice. She owned herself, from her age; her gender; her religion; her background; her Eva-blue, polyester pantsuits; her hatred of ripped jeans; her love of Chicken McNuggets and dislike of "fancy" restaurants. She never covered up her tattoo—just the opposite. She used it to start conversations, whether with museum visitors or food servers at restaurants, with flight attendants or fellow travelers seated next to her. There was never a time in her life when she didn't think it appropriate to tell people that she was an Auschwitz survivor and that she had forgiven the Nazis. Her fierce protection of her right to be who she was and do what she believed in underlay all of her accomplishments, as she continued to speak about the Holocaust and her forgiveness of the Nazis, even as she experienced backlash. Her authenticity was another quality that endeared her to others, especially young people.

Perhaps the most unexpected thing about Eva was her sense of humor. Eva was a naturally funny person, sometimes for just being so Eva, but often with a purpose. The Holocaust is a very dark subject, difficult to discuss in any circumstances. As with her clothing, she used humor to help people relax, to make it easier to ask questions, to have a conversation, letting people know she was comfortable sharing the details of both the difficult and the happy aspects of her life.

Alex Kor, Eva's son, has many stories about his mom's sense of humor. In 1984, Eva decided to visit Auschwitz by herself. The family was very concerned for her safety on that long trip. Eva went anyway, everything went fine, and she had sweatshirts made for Alex and his sister, Rina. On the front of the sweatshirts was the liberation picture of Eva and Miriam, and on the back it said, "My mom survived Auschwitz and all I got was this lousy sweatshirt."

On the 50th anniversary of liberation, Eva was leading a group of people to visit Auschwitz, and Alex joined the group. On arrival, Eva was told the camp wasn't going to let her in because she didn't have the paperwork necessary for the tour bus. She marched to the front of the bus, pulled up her sleeve, pointed to her tattoo, and said, "Fifty years ago, you wouldn't let me out. And now you won't let me in?" They got in that day.

How could an Auschwitz survivor make jokes about the Holocaust? By being a survivor who forgave everyone who had hurt her, healing her own unfathomable emotional pain. From all accounts of Terre Haute residents, Eva was an angry and bitter woman before she forgave; all agreed that she seemed to be a very different person afterward.

Eva began leading visits to Auschwitz in 1985 and continued to the end of her life. It is impossible to fully prepare to tour Auschwitz; it is a mentally and emotionally grueling, though profound, experience. And while Eva gave it all the weight and darkness it deserves, she never let tour members stay in that deep, dark hole. "Why are you crying?" she would ask a group member in tears. "I'm not crying. I am alive and happy. Your job is to learn what happened here and to be a witness, to make the world a better place when you go home. That is how you respond to the knowledge and insight you have gained here. You don't need to cry."

Indeed, her right to be a victorious survivor rather than a suffering victim was always front and center at Auschwitz. In the summer of 2007, a tourist in Block 6 in Auschwitz confronted Eva and members of her tour group who were taking pictures of Eva with her image from the 1945 liberation photo, which is displayed on a wall. The tourist declared, "This is not appropriate. You shouldn't be laughing, taking pictures, smiling." Eva immediately pointed to herself and said, "That little girl is me, and I've earned the right to smile." By the end of the exchange, the tourist was smiling and crying, which earned her further admonishment from Eva, accompanied by a hug.

Eva embraced joy in many ways, from the simple plea-sures of witnessing budding trees in the spring, seeing family and friends, to her daily work at the museum. Her joy also included some mischievousness, as seen when she was in Al-buquerque for a teacher's conference. A just-married couple were having their photos taken in the hotel hallway. Eva saw it as an opportunity to photobomb the shoot while wearing a bowler hat and a mustache she "borrowed" from the pho-tographer's props. During the making of a documentary on her life, Eva and the crew took a trip to Israel, during which the group decided to take an impromptu trip to the Dead Sea. Everyone but Eva had brought shorts or swim clothes, but that was not going to be a problem. She waded out into the water in her blue pantsuit, floating in the sea, and loving every minute of it. The little woman had style.

Another unexpected delight about Eva was her success on social media; she particularly loved Twitter. It could be said that she lived to tweet. The subjects were endless—advice, reflections, memories, questions. Eva's tweets were wide-ranging and completely unpredictable, as she herself could be. Here are some highlights:

1/15/17:
My top 5 ways to fight winter blues:
5. Be among happy friends
4. Work on great projects
3. Eat good pizza
2. Dream of spring
1. Try Florida!

In 2018, Eva was named the Grand Marshal of the Indy 500 car race, where she bonded with Nikki Sixx of the heavy metal band, Motley Crue. Of course, Eva started a Twitter exchange afterward. From Eva to Nikki:

@nikkiSixx, It was nice to meet you on the red carpet at Indianapolis 500. What could I do to become a rock star like you? Eva.

Nikki's response: *"Eva my sweetheart you've been a rock star your whole life. Thank you for inspiring so many."*

12/28/18:
Eva responded to a tweet sent by her son, supposedly showing the foot of Shaquille O'Neal:
Hey Shaq: I think my feet are cuter than yours, and I have more mileage on them.

12/24/18:
So amazed to live in the USA. Although I am Jewish, I enjoy the wonderful Christmas season when many observe the religious meaning of Christmas, but we can enjoy the spirit of hope, giving, peace and goodwill—all religions can join in.

12/26/18
I forgot to share with you one of the fun things my children used to do before Christmas and Hanukkah.

We would bake cookies both Jewish and Christian and put them on plates and deliver them to friends and neighbors—it was a lot of fun for children and me too!

1/23/19
"One of the biggest challenges when we study the tragedy of Auschwitz is to understand that the perpetrators were not monsters. They were people—fathers, husbands, and dog owners—who accepted the ideology of hatred and evil and were able to do monstrous things on its behalf."

Eva's biggest splash on social media was an interview produced by Buzzfeed. A 15-minute video of the interview was posted on the Buzzfeed Facebook page and garnered over 200 million views and over a million shares. She was already known in several countries in Europe, but the Buzzfeed video provided her with truly international fame. She began to be recognized nearly every place she went, and she relished her new fame's benefit of being upgraded on flights.

The last years of Eva's life had many other joys. One of the biggest was a documentary, *Eva: A-7063*, released in 2018 and produced by Ted Green films and the Indianapolis PBS station, WFYI. It offers important context to Eva's story, particularly during the middle years of her life, when she struggled with anger, bitterness, and rejection. The film was shown on PBS stations across the U.S. and in Germany, won numerous awards, and has been widely used by teachers, along with this book.

Another special friendship bloomed when Scottish musician Raymond Meade read Eva's story and contacted her. The BBC produced a documentary about Eva's story and their friendship, captured in Eva's tweet on 1/27/19:

> *"You are a very special person to me too. When we reach out to each other—we connect we touch each other's heart—and that is magic. So let's reach out to each other and create good magic in the world."*

Because Eva had not always been treated well in her home state, especially in her early years, Eva was especially proud when she was bestowed with the highest honor given to an Indiana citizen, the Sachem Award, by Governor Eric Holcomb. However, in her acceptance speech she revealed bigger political ambition. She wanted to address Congress in Washington, D.C. so she could give them a good telling off, and insist they stop bickering and get some things done. She was convinced that she could set those politicians straight.

More recognition came when Eva was asked to participate in a Shoah Foundation project. The exhibit includes hologram-like technology that enables visitors to interact in question-and-answer form with 3D videos of Holocaust survivors. Creating her testimony required Eva to sit inside a room for an entire week with hundreds of lights shining on her, surrounded by cameras, answering over a thousand questions about the various aspects of her life. The recorded testimonies of the survivors can be found in several Holocaust museums in the country, in addition to the Shoah Foundation in Los Angeles.

Eva also received an award from the Anti-Defamation League at the John F. Kennedy Center in Washington, D.C., for her efforts in Holocaust education. Though Eva continued to share her story and her message of forgiveness knowing many did not agree with her, she had always hoped for acceptance from the Jewish and Holocaust communities. Her only annoyance at the Kennedy Center award was the five-minute limit on her speech. Getting Eva to speak was easy; sometimes getting her to stop was not.

Eva's thoughts were broad and deep until the end of her life. Her lectures continued to lengthen, because the "life lessons" she wanted to teach young people continued to multiply. And her interests broadened—she didn't just challenge others to continue thinking of how to make their world a better place, it was a constant process for her, particularly helping young people. She wanted traumatized kids and young adults to have a chance to live on a farm as she did in Israel, healed by the community and the work of gardening and taking care of animals. At school events, she never failed to insist that school uniforms should be worn by all kids—they would look nicer and would prevent students from being judged, for good or bad, on their clothing. The importance she placed on clothing was evident in many situations, perhaps stemming from the warm memories of her mother's care for what her daughters wore.

Eva Mozes Kor died in the early morning hours of July 4, 2019. She had expressed many times that she wanted to live to 110 to be present at the 100th anniversary commemoration event for the Auschwitz liberation. On one hand, she was 85 and had health issues that had put her in the hospital several times in 2019. Yet she was still going, traveling the world, giving lectures, guiding the tours, accepting awards, working away in the office in her museum. And if ever there was someone who could survive by sheer determination, it was Eva Kor.

On the Auschwitz group trips that summer, she had been happy and doing well, guiding the museum groups, with nothing to indicate she was in the last days of her life. She tweeted out her delight in finding her favorite food nearby: "Can you believe that today I can get Chicken McNuggets near Auschwitz? That would have been wonderful 75 years ago. They taste the same in every country and were delicious." Her death was sudden and unexpected at that point, and there were many people, with her and around the world, who were devastated by her loss. The media coverage was extensive.

In a way it was fitting that Eva died on the 4th of July. She represented the promise and diversity in immigrants, how they can enrich our lives and our culture in ways we might not expect. As with many immigrants, she was fiercely proud to be an American citizen. She had worked to get her citizenship, and was appreciative of our freedoms and culture, as reflected in her tweets. While it was Soviet soldiers who liberated Auschwitz, she always spoke of seeing planes with an American flag on them that gave her hope and how, even then, she associated the American flag with freedom.

The fact that she died in Krakow, the city closest to Auschwitz, was troubling to some. They thought it tragic that she would die there, after braving so much to survive when she was a child. On the other hand, there were fitting aspects of the place of her death. To Eva, Auschwitz was a place of triumph, the biggest of her life. She, a small child, had beaten the Nazis. As she always said, "The Nazis are dead. I am alive." Indeed, it was noticeable to others that she almost seemed the most alive and happy when visiting the camp. In a way, she celebrated her life each time she returned. But those trips were not without dark moments. Eva always laid flowers and lit a candle in honor of her family at the camp, and it was still emotional for her all those years later. The loss of her mother, in particular, was a pain that never completely went away.

Eva Kor, the humanitarian, the fighter for justice, for healing, for peace, was in a way formed in that camp, a woman of strength and single-minded determination. While much of her life she did not believe in God—which is very common among Holocaust survivors—her views had changed in the years before her death. She expressed to several that she thought God could exist and perhaps she was meant to go through what she did, and to discover the healing power of forgiveness and spread that message around the world.

The last day of her life, Eva was just outside the Auschwitz grounds when she received a text message from trip coordinator and close friend, Beth Nairn, telling her that thirty-six handsome young men were waiting to see her and wanted to sing for her. Eva arrived a few minutes later to find a boys' choir. She requested her favorite song, "The Impossible Dream," the lyrics expressing her belief that anything is possible. Somehow, the choir director and boys found the words and sang a bit followed by two other beautiful songs they had rehearsed, and she thoroughly enjoyed their performance.

She also had plans to visit the Katowice convent for the first time since her stay there after liberation, but alas, that was not to be. Staff of her museum had visited a few days beforehand to verify the location before taking Eva on the trip. In an incredible coincidence, the nuns wore habits, currently and in 1945, of the same bright blue she had adopted as her color later in life. On seeing photos of the nuns, she agreed that the blue she loved might have been a forgotten association with freedom and safety. She also met Rabbi Bleich, Vice President of the Jewish World Congress, and when Eva explained her forgiveness, he asked her if she had forgiven only on her own behalf or for others. She assured him that she had only forgiven on her own behalf, and he told her he thought her forgiveness was fine. She declared that she liked him.

Eva died in the early morning hours of July 4th, having had a prominent Jewish rabbi give his blessing on her forgiveness, a personal performance by a boys choir, and doing what she loved most—leading the group through Auschwitz, telling her story, feeling gratitude and joy, and sharing her message of forgiveness to heal the world.

When the documentary maker, Ted Green, was interviewing Governor Holcomb for the film, he asked the governor to envision the scene if ever Eva had her wish and was invited to speak to Congress. Governor Holcomb responded, "Well, there would be one giant in the room, and it would be Eva." Without a doubt, the governor was right. Eva Mozes Kor was one of the giants of our times.

Eva used to tell children and teens that they had the power to change the world. She understood that people, young and old, think they have to be part of a big organization to make change on a broad scale. But what Eva taught us, by words and deed, is the power of the individual.

If a 4'9" Auschwitz survivor, orphan, refugee, immigrant, realtor with a Romanian accent in Terre Haute, Indiana, can find a worldwide audience for her story and her message, any one of us can make a difference, whoever and wherever we are.

Eva always ended her lectures by saying, "Anger is a seed for war; forgiveness is a seed for peace." I hope readers will be inspired to choose peace, in honor of the one, and surely the only, Eva Mozes Kor.

Peggy Porter Tierney
Publisher, Editor
Board Chair Emeritas, CANDLES Holocaust Museum

24. *Peace Learning Center, Indianapolis, IN*

25. *Eva's peace garden dedication, Newfields, Indianapolis, IN*

26. *Eva with Governor Eric Holcomb*

ACKNOWLEDGMENTS

The publisher would like to thank the following people for their help with this new edition: Alex Kor, Ted Green, Beth Nairn, Michael Woerle, Markus Goldbach, and to those who also continue working to keep Eva's legacy alive: Governor Eric Holcomb, John Abrams, Erin White, CANDLES Holocaust Museum, and the Indiana Historical Society.

Author's Note

Lisa Rojany Buccieri
April 2009

This book came about through the efforts of many people. First and foremost, *Surviving the Angel of Death: The Story of a Mengele Twin in Auschwitz* is based on one person's memory. Eva Mozes Kor is an eyewitness to a multitude of crimes against humanity. Through her lectures at schools and in the Holocaust museum she founded, Eva always knew that her story was an important one for young people to learn. When Peggy Tierney first approached her about publishing a book for young adults, she agreed immediately. Eva's greatest dream is that her book will be used in schools to teach young people about the Holocaust and be inspired to use its lessons in their own lives.

Katie McKy interviewed Eva extensively, asking many pertinent questions and getting Eva to open up and express herself in ways that young people could relate to.

Susan Goldman Rubin wrote an extensive, detailed out-line, both meeting Eva in person and adding much valuable, insightful research to the materials drawn from.

Peggy Tierney, our editor at Tanglewood Books, has served as Eva's cheerleader for years through several writers and too many drafts to count. She knew Eva had an impor-tant story to tell and she believed that it needed to be told. I want to thank Peggy for believing in my ability to take these materials and write this book in a way that both adheres to the truth as Eva recalls it and also brings her story to life so that young readers can relive it in the safety of these pages. I can only hope that those readers find this book worth all our efforts.

It has been my privilege to work on this important proj-ect, helping to pass on Eva Mozes Kor's story to a new gen-eration of readers. There are not many children of the Ho-locaust, much less many of the Mengele twins, who lived to tell their stories. Eva did. And this story is told in her voice, in the first person, as an adult looking back over sixty-five years, to a time when a little girl, clutching the trembling hand of her identical twin sister, showed up at the gates of horror—and survived.

Author Biographies

 Eva Mozes Kor was a resident of Terre Haute, Indiana, for 59 years, where she was a successful realtor. She founded an organization for surviving Mengele twins in 1985, and helped to pressure governments to search for Josef Mengele. In 1995, she opened a small Holocaust museum in Terre Haute, which grew into the CANDLES Holocaust Museum and Education Center, where she gave many presentations and talks, especially to groups of school children. She was a recognized speaker, both nationally and internationally, on topics related to the Holocaust, medical ethics, forgiveness, and peace. She was covered in numerous media outlets, including "60 Minutes" and "20/20," and is the subject of a documentary, *Eva: A-7063*. She died on July 4, 2019, in Krakow, Poland, during a group trip to Auschwitz.

Lisa Rojany Buccieri has written over 100 children's books, including several award-winning and bestselling titles. She is also a publishing executive and editor with over 20 years of experience in the industry, and is the lead writer for *Writing Children's Books for Dummies*. As well as spearheading four publishing startups, Lisa has simultaneously run her own business, Editorial Services of L.A. She has been Editorial/Publishing Director for Golden Books, Price Stern Sloan/Penguin Group USA, Intervisual Books, Gateway Learning Corp (Hooked on Phonics), and Intervisual Books. Lisa lives with her family in Los Angeles. She may be contacted at www.EditorialServicesofLA.com

Photo Credits

1. Map from Yad Vashem, The World Holocaust Remembrance Center.
2. Detail of map above, with line between the Şimleu Silvaniei ghetto and Auschwitz added.
3. From Eva Kor's private collection.
4. From Eva Kor's private collection.
5. From Eva Kor's private collection.
6. From Eva Kor's private collection.
7. From Eva Kor's private collection.
8. Courtesy of the United States Holocaust Memorial Museum.
9. Courtesy of the United States Holocaust Memorial Museum.
10. Courtesy of State Museum Auschwitz-Birkenau in Oświęcim, Poland.
11. Courtesy of the United States Holocaust Memorial Museum.

12. Courtesy of Yad Vashem, The World Holocaust
    Remembrance Center. Photographer: Wilhelm
    Brasse. Horizontal black bar added.
13. Courtesy of State Museum Auschwitz-Birkenau
    in Oświęcim, Poland.
14. A photo taken of an original document in State
    Museum Auschwitz-Birkenau archives, from Eva
    Kor's private collection.
15. Photo of document from Eva Kor's private
    collection.
16. Courtesy of State Museum Auschwitz-Birkenau
    in Oświęcim, Poland.
17. From Eva Kor's private collection.
18. Courtesy of the United States Holocaust
    Memorial Museum.
19. From Eva Kor's private collection.
20. From Eva Kor's private collection.
21. From Eva Kor's private collection.
22. From Eva Kor's private collection.
23. From Eva Kor's private collection.
24. Courtesy of Ted Green Films and WFYI.
25. Courtesy of Ted Green Films and WFYI.
26. Courtesy of Ted Green Films and WFYI.

The views or opinions expressed in this book, and the
context in which the images are used, do not necessarily
reflect the views or policy of, nor imply approval or endorse-
ment by, the United States Holocaust Memorial Museum.

Additional Resources

Learn more about the documentary and related materials at: www.thestoryofeva.com

Visit Eva's museum online:
www.candlesholocaustmuseum.org